WILLPOWER

Regain Your Self-Control and Rediscover Your Willpower Instinct

Allison Perry

Allison Perry

PO Box 303

Bolivia, NC 28422

ap@allisonperrybooks.com

www.AllisonPerryBooks.com

Limits of Liability and Disclaimer of Warranty

Warning – Disclaimer

This book is dedicated to my son, Malcolm, who shows me every day the incredible things that can happen when you tap into your willpower instinct.

ALSO BY ALLISON PERRY

Small Talk: Discover Topics, Tips and How to Effortlessly Connect With Anyone

Table of Contents

Introduction

In the absence of willpower the most complete collection of virtues and talents is wholly worthless. ~ Aleister Crowley

Willpower. It's at the center of mythical legends and heroic tales the world over. It's what causes the hero to keep pushing through trials and tribulations. It's what gives the heroine her ability to persevere. We marvel at these stories of incredible men and women - at people who seem to effortlessly exert self-control no matter how trying the circumstances – and we wonder how to tap into our own willpower instinct.

Intuitively, we know we need more willpower in our lives. We talk obsessively about dieting, building our savings, beating procrastination, and achieving our long held dreams…and then we talk about it some more. We just can't seem to bridge the gap from wanting willpower….to actually mastering the skill.

This book will give you the power to bridge that gap.

You'll discover the fascinating research that has been conducted on willpower, what scientists have recently discovered about self-control, and how that knowledge can help you in your own life.

We will explore what willpower really is, why it's so elusive, and the best and easiest ways to tap into your willpower instinct.

We will also show you a step by step process you can use to immediately gain more willpower and effortlessly maintain it in the future.

After all, simply understanding how willpower works won't help you master it. You must know how to apply it in your own life. You need to know that when the book is closed, and you're faced with a looming deadline, a delicious piece of chocolate cake, or a challenging obstacle in your path, that you will have the knowledge AND the skills to forge ahead with confidence and purpose.

This is the critical piece missing in so many books – and the most important. Because of all the skills you can master in your life, willpower is the most crucial.

In 2011, The American Psychological Association conducted a survey asking folks what was holding them back from improving their lives. Lack of willpower was cited by people as the number one reason for not being able to make important changes in their lives.

Willpower is what will determine the level of success you achieve. More than intelligence, more than knowledge, more than who you know – your ability to stick to something, to stay focused and persevere – that is what will determine the quality of your life.

With the right amount of self-discipline, you can easily accomplish what you set out to do. You can make healthy dietary choices, exercise regularly, be financially fit, build a nest egg, pursue your dream job, start a business, stop procrastinating, and achieve all sorts of life-changing goals.

Willpower is what will make it happen. Willpower will bridge the gap between where you are now…and where you want to be.

Are you ready to tap into your willpower instinct?

Let's get started!

What is Willpower?

Self-control is self-mastery. It is kingship over all life. At the center of your being sits yourself. Your seat ought to be a throne. If you are not in control, if there are any forces in your nature that are unruly, that do not acknowledge your sway, you are not the king you should be. Part of your kingdom is in insurrection. The strength of your life is divided. The strong man is he whose whole being is subject to him.

~ *James Russell Miller, The Beauty of Self-Control, 1911*

Do you remember when you were a kid sitting at the dinner table? Do you remember your mom's favorite line: "You can have your dessert after you finish your broccoli." Man, was it hard to finish that broccoli! But, we powered through and managed to make it to that dessert.

Or, after school, it was, "Finish your homework, and then you can watch television." Some of us actually dove in and strove to make our work correct. Some of us did our homework as quickly as possible, leaving many errors, in order to watch TV. And some of us just ignored our homework and went out to play instead. (Sorry mom!)

Today, as adults, it has become even more difficult to abstain from pleasure-seeking activities that offer such sweet short-term rewards. In a society where stress is at an all-time high, willpower can be a tough trait to find - and a seemingly impossible one to harness.

As a society, we are overweight, in debt, and killing ourselves with our bad habits. Sometimes, it feels like we just don't have any willpower at all.

To make it even worse, we are inundated with tantalizing distractions and temptations in today's modern society. Smartphones run our lives with a thousand applications, advertisements crowd our commutes, television and a couch beckon to us after work, and a pantry full of premade meals and cheap junk food make it easy to quickly find a tasty treat.

At the end of a tough day filled with hard financial choices, trying to eat healthy with barely enough time to cook, and trying to avoid ingrained bad habits, we're exhausted. It makes it all too easy to veg out on the couch, pick up that box of cookies and just eat one, or two, or several. Sometimes it just seems easier to give up.

So what is this elusive thing called willpower and why does it seem to run out just when we need it the most? Can it be controlled? Can we get more of it? Or are we just allotted a certain amount in our lifetime?

In the dictionary, willpower is defined as control of one's impulses and actions; our self-control. Willpower, as defined by famous researcher Roy F. Baumeister, is the adequacy of a person's strength to overcome an unwanted impulse, feeling, or thought.

In practical terms, willpower is considered the single biggest contributor to a successful life. Willpower is consistently cited as something that most people yearn for but seldom understand.

Contrary to popular belief, willpower is not something that a few lucky ones are blessed with; we all have the willpower instinct – we all have the ability to tap into its power.

This book will help you understand the willpower instinct, what it is, what barriers you will face, how habits play a part in the process, and effective ways to set goals that you can easily achieve.

Ultimately, willpower is about creating a better quality of life and that is what this book focuses on: how to avoid short-term temptations and delay immediate gratifications to meet long-term goals.

For example, try telling yourself that you have two choices. You can reward yourself with a piece of cake every night for eating well the entire day, or you can reward yourself with a full day of eating whatever you want after two weeks of eating well.

Which sounds more rewarding?

Which one will help you achieve your goal of healthy living?

The second choice might have been more difficult, but you managed to hold off on junk food and eat healthy for two weeks. The first may have been easier, but you had fourteen pieces of cake over a two-week period.

This is similar to the test that Angela Duckworth, PhD, and Martin Seligman, PhD, conducted with eighth graders to test their self-control. They found that students who ranked high in self-control were the students who could wait a week for two dollars after answering a simple questionnaire. The ones who ranked lower were the ones who wanted one dollar right away.

The same study shows that the students with higher self-control were better students, ranked higher on standardized tests, stayed out of trouble, and were in better physical shape. It turns out that the more we practice self-control in our youth, the easier it will be to exhibit willpower as adults. (Parents take note!)

But that doesn't mean that we can't build up our willpower as adults—we shouldn't give up. In the next few chapters, we'll delve into what stands in our way of making healthy choices and the barriers we need to overcome to tap into our willpower.

For now, it's important to just become aware of how you currently use willpower in your life. Take a moment to evaluate yourself, the choices you make, and the habits you have developed.

Do you reward yourself often? Or do you work harder while you wait for a bigger payout?

Do you mindlessly grab a bag of chips when you get home? Or do you make a conscious choice to stop by the gym after work?

Do you get to work on that online business you've wanted to start? Or do you find yourself surfing the net, getting lost in Facebook or Pinterest?

When evaluating your "less than desirable" behavior, take a close look at any patterns that may be contributing to your bad habits.

Let's say you are someone who is trying to lose a few pounds. Are there times in the day that you seem more prone to struggle with snacking? Is that 10:00 am attack of the munchies too much to resist? Or is it that time around 2:30 in the afternoon when you start to feel sluggish and head to the vending machine or chocolate stash to give you a little boost of energy?

If you are interested in creating a business but just can't seem to get started, track how you are currently using your time. Do you automatically go straight to Facebook when you get on your computer? Do you have a habit of checking your email every time you pick up your phone? Look at what patterns currently exist in your life to see where or when you struggle most with tapping into your willpower.

For instance, here's a common scenario for many folks. You set your New Year's resolutions. You have only the best of intentions. You start off strong. You are tracking your progress toward your goal. The first week is great! The second week you're still doing great. Week three is okay, but a little bit of the initial excitement is gone.

By the end of week 4, you start to wane a little bit from your goal. You cheat a little on your workout routine. Maybe you hit the snooze button one too many times, and skip the morning run you'd been going on each morning. Or maybe you decide to watch your favorite reality show or the recorded shows on the DVR instead of working diligently on the novel you started to write.

While none of these things is inherently a bad thing to do, it's when these little things stop being temporary that it becomes an issue. Problems arise when the temporary "hiccups" in your routine become the norm rather than the exception.

This is why it's crucial that you become aware of your choices throughout the day, no matter how uncomfortable it might make you feel.

It can be hard to put ourselves under a microscope, particularly if the results are less than flattering. However, becoming aware of our actions can help us take the next step toward achieving our goals. This is one of the reasons why it's necessary to track our progress when we set goals. When we are aware of how much, or how little, we are accomplishing, we can try to find ways to improve our results.

History of Willpower

Now that we've covered the very basics of willpower, let's talk briefly about the history of willpower. It's important to see how it has evolved, and how modern society plays a part in how we view it in our lives.

As far back as the Humanist movement in France, control of one's self has been considered a science that can be studied and manipulated. Back then, it was believed that men could gain esteem by gaining self-control.

This idea started to appear in the United States around the nineteenth century during the Industrial Revolution. As machines became more prevalent in our lives, scientists began studying the "human machine." They believed that willpower could be harnessed as a type of fuel for life.

During the Industrial Revolution, a man's moral resistance and strength of will, his ability to avoid temptations, measured the worth of a man. It was from this belief that the idea of the power suit originated.

But just like willpower peters out in our own lives, it seemed to dwindle in history as well. We just seemed to run out of it during the Progressive Movement in the early twentieth century. While a select few men with ironclad wills rose to the top, the masses that were left behind looked for reasons why. They started to blame their external environment for their lot in life.

For example, a person who became involved in crime later in life, or a person who lived in poverty, could blame their environment instead of their lack of self-control for their poor situation.

A few decades later, the Nazis released a propaganda film called Triumph of the Will by Leni Riefenstahl. It recounted several Nazi successes paired with carefully selected speeches by Adolf Hitler. One of the main themes of the film was power. During the film, Hitler is heard saying, "It is our will that this state and this Reich shall endure through the coming millennia."

The world quickly shifted from blaming their surroundings for their lack of willpower to not wanting any willpower—not if it resembled the kind of willpower the Nazis seemed to have. Suddenly willpower was a bad word. It was undying and scary, and tied to one goal: domination. Willpower gained many negative connotations thanks to this film and thanks to World War II.

After the War, willpower was pushed to the background as Americans became immersed in the booming consumer culture. To large companies, willpower and self-control were bad for business. Consumers purchased goods, unbridled from the staunch and rigid ways of wartime.

Shortly after that, Norman Vincent Peale wrote The Power of Positive Thinking. The book focused on how to achieve fulfillment by thinking positive thoughts. This began the movement toward the Law of Attraction and the belief that our thoughts create our reality. While filled with valuable insight, the role of willpower was largely forgotten in these works.

The pendulum has finally swung in the opposite direction. Psychologists have been launching a revival of interest in the concept of willpower. In studies, they have shown that not only is willpower a real and enormously potent energy, but that one's belief in it need not put you in the ranks of a cruel leader like Hitler (greater self-control is actually linked to greater levels of empathy) and that one's belief in it need not involve blaming someone for their misfortunes (external factors can, and do, play a part in our lives). The research also offers compelling evidence of the role that willpower plays in determining the quality of our lives.

Psychologists have recently found that certain characteristics correlate with positive life outcomes and choices. Consistently, psychologists agree that people with higher levels of happiness, health, and success have one thing in common: willpower.

They also agree that willpower is a trait we control. Knowing this, we can start to take steps to improve our lives with goals we can actually accomplish. We can procrastinate less and have less stress while making better choices that lead to more positive outcomes.

Now that we have a good grasp on what willpower is, it's time to move into a deeper understanding of the subject; why it can seem to be hard to access or control, and the secret to making almost effortless change. So use that willpower instinct and keep reading! We're just getting started.

Why Is Willpower So Elusive?

That majestic endowment [the Will] constitutes the high privilege granted to each man apparently to test how much the man will make of himself. It is clothed with powers which will enable him to obtain the greatest of all possessions—self-possession. Self-possession implies the capacity for self-restraint, self-compulsion and self-direction; and he who has these, if he live long enough, can have any other possession that he wants.

~ William Hanna Thompson, Brain and Personality, 1906

While willpower can be an incredibly powerful force in our lives, it can also be rather elusive. Obviously, this creates a problem. Our lack of self-control keeps us from producing the change we want to see in our lives. While we could use this lack as an excuse for our poor choices and stay stuck in our present situation, a better option is to discover what's keeping us from using our willpower and how we can overcome it.

After decades of being pushed to the background, it's time to bring willpower front and center and actively embrace it in our lives.

I want you to think back to when you were in school, a few weeks before a big paper was due. You're looking around the classroom as your teacher explains the project and you see a poster on the wall that says, "Beware: Due dates are closer than they appear."

You scoff and think to yourself that you aren't going to get caught in the procrastination trap. You're going to work ahead and get your paper finished right on time.

To reward yourself for having this brilliant plan, you go home and watch your favorite movie. Once that's over, you decide to go play some basketball. Now that you've exercised some, you're too tired to work on your paper, so you go to sleep. And the next day, the process repeats.

We've all been there. We've all avoided projects until the very last minute and then had to cram weeks of work into just a few days, or even just a few hours.

But it doesn't stop there. Think back to the excuse you might have given to your teacher for the low quality of your work. You might have said that it was because you didn't have enough passion for the topic. It could have been that you didn't have enough time to properly express yourself.

Maybe you told her that you were never taught how to manage your time well or control your thoughts well enough to put them onto paper. Or you might have been honest and told your teacher that you procrastinated.

All of the excuses you gave your teacher were barriers to help you improve your paper, to access your willpower, and in the long-term, to help you improve your life. Excuses are one of the most common barriers to increasing willpower.

I don't have the money.

I don't have the resources or the connections.

I don't have the knowledge or the skills.

One of the most common excuses we tell ourselves is that we just need more time. We've all wished for another day to finish our work, or a few more hours to polish a project, or a little bit longer to relax and catch a break.

This is another barrier that we throw up to avoid change. The reality is that we all have the same number of hours in the day. It's our ability to tap into our willpower that makes all the difference.

No matter what your excuse (and we all have them), it's important that you start to be aware of what excuses really are; simply a way to avoid an impending challenge and get you off the hook.

When we throw up excuses, our willpower doesn't even come into play. Our brain has already registered the fact that we don't have what we need to accomplish the task. Why even tap into our willpower when there's nothing to be done? We have already lost the battle.

Excuses will always act as a barrier to tapping into your willpower instinct. Perhaps the most devastating excuse of all is this: believing that willpower is an inherited trait rather than a learned skill. If we convince ourselves that willpower can't be learned, we can convince ourselves that we can't be taught.

This is the biggest barrier to tapping into your willpower instinct. It's easy to make an excuse and say, "Well, I can't be taught. I'll just have to live like this." That simply isn't the case. We need to approach the subject from a different angle.

Research has clearly shown that we all have willpower and self-control. It's why I constantly refer to it as an instinct; as a reminder that it's something we all share, an innate part of the human experience. So the question shouldn't be, "Can willpower be learned?" It should be, "How can my willpower be strengthened?" When you approach willpower with this attitude, the barriers to accessing your willpower melt away.

Of course, accessing your willpower isn't enough. We need to understand how it works, how much we have, and how we can generate more. In the next chapter, we'll dive into those questions and uncover some startling new research on the ways willpower works.

Can We Increase Our Willpower Reserve?

Don't let mental blocks control you. Set yourself free. Confront your fear and turn the mental blocks into building blocks.

~ Roopleen, Words to inspire the winner in YOU

"Just Do It!" is perhaps the most recognized statement regarding willpower. The question that hasn't been answered for us, though, is how exactly should we "just do it?"

Psychologists have pondered the same question for decades. Years of research and subsequent studies have left us with even more interesting questions: is willpower a limited resource? If yes, then what makes it that way? What exactly stands in our way when we try to harness the full potential of our willpower?

The subject is a vast and fascinating one, and more importantly, relevant to us in an age when obesity, alcoholism, and drug addiction have skyrocketed. The related medical expenses cost millions of dollars and the health and fitness industry markets shiny new products to desperate weight watchers trying to work off those extra pounds.

There is also a huge market of make money online products and business opportunities being marketed to the masses. For many, the desire to tap into the latest hot business trend is too hard to resist. They get caught in an endless cycle of buying products, starting projects, and then moving onto the next idea before ever experiencing success or completing an info course.

Let's face it. If willpower were easy, we'd all be millionaires with healthy, toned bodies.

So why does willpower require so much effort?

Let's think about it this way. Imagine a child sitting at a table staring at a chocolate pie who has been told not to eat it. Now, sitting at a table doesn't require much physical effort, and neither does eating a pie, but refraining from digging into the pie requires an internal process that is much more painstaking than the physical act of sitting or eating. That internal process is willpower.

Scientists have discovered that willpower behaves just like any other form of energy in our body. It gets depleted and consumed like everything else.

Think back to that paper from Chapter Two. One of the things you may have done to catch up from procrastination was to stay up all night. It takes a lot of rest to recover from that. Willpower works the same way. After we've exhausted our willpower, we need time to replenish our supply. ✱

According to Mark Muraven and Roy F. Baumeister, two renowned psychologists, people have to exert self-control in order to curb their desires, or "delay gratification." So when we are placed in a situation where we have to use our willpower, we have to consciously overcome our desires and urges even though that may be the opposite of what we want to do.

We're "swimming against the tide" of our own desires.

In order to better explain the finite nature of willpower, a basic understanding of Muraven and Baumeister's model is necessary. First, it says that willpower is required to make decisions, take initiative, and exert control.

We feel dozens of desires and urges in a day. Our supply of willpower gets used up not only when we face those urges, but also when we have to make decisions against them. A craving (the desire) uses up your willpower, but deciding to wait until lunchtime instead of snacking right now (the decision) uses up even more of your willpower. It's a downward spiral of urges and decisions sapping up your limited willpower strength until it wears down.

This was clearly shown in a recent study where participants were given beepers that beeped at random intervals; they had to record their exact responses at the time the beeper sounded. The study showed that most people experienced some form of desire at the precise moment of each beep, and, on average, people spent four hours a day resisting those desires.

There's a countless list of trivial, everyday choices we face, such as which route to take to school or work, how much money to spend or not spend, whether to take a nap or finish an impending project, and so on. Add to that the multitude of desires we resist, such as focusing on work instead of playing on Facebook, eating fruit instead of candy, biting our tongue when we'd rather yell at someone. These choices and desires constantly work against us, draining our supply of willpower.

Second, the model states that a person has a limited capacity for willpower and that this capacity can easily get depleted. This is called "ego depletion." Most researchers agree that willpower is a finite resource; if used too often, we run out of it.

This means that a person can't control all of his urges at the same time, because his capacity for willpower diminishes after frequent use. This is because all efforts that require willpower use the same "pool of resources." So, directing your efforts toward one goal diminishes the resources available for another goal.

Imagine you have a jar marked "willpower." This jar starts out full, but each desire you resist and decision you make uses up some of the willpower. Eventually the jar will run out, at which point you have to send it back to the "store" for a refill.

This illustrates the point that we need to give ourselves a break from the stress of urges and decisions in order to relax our minds and replenish our capacity for willpower.

For instance, imagine you had a very stressful day at work, and you resisted the urge to scream at your annoying coworker who kept making mistakes that you had to fix. Suppose you had also just started a diet and given up caffeine. All of these things require an active amount of willpower.

So, imagine after a long day of working hard to avoid all of these things, your child starts whining for a toy at the grocery store. For many of us, our willpower supply would be completely depleted and we would end up giving in just to avoid the battle. Or, we would completely lose it and yell and scream because we had no willpower left to handle the situation properly.

This is how ego depletion works. Unlike our other mental capabilities like memory, where we have a limitless reserve, there is a finite amount of willpower available for our use.

This is exactly the psychology that marketers are tapping into when they place small convenience items, like candy and soda, at the checkout line. There is a reason it's called the "impulse aisle."

Marketers know we have just spent our time walking around the store, making choices that test our willpower: Do I get the cereal that tastes good, or the one with less sugar? Do I get the generic chicken to save money, or get the brand name?

By the time we check out, we're worn down (especially if we're shopping with children). We exhibit poor impulse control. Our willpower is depleted, and we can't resist the urge to buy that candy bar or bag of chips, tempting us as we wait in line.

What Muraven and Baumeister concluded from their model, and what is now a widely accepted notion, is that willpower behaves like a muscle. Someone whose willpower is "out of shape" will need to work harder than others to get their self-control back into optimal form.

While this is happening, the willpower muscle might feel sore and exhausted. Like any other muscle, building it up to achieve its maximum potential takes time and patience.

It is worth noting, however, that if a person is unable to rest and regenerate their strength due to stressful circumstances, then they may be left permanently lacking in these resources, which will ultimately weaken their self-control.

For instance, a physical laborer who works double shifts while dealing with a difficult foreman at work, a demanding wife and family at home, and a nonexistent social network, will most likely become short-tempered and harsh as his strained circumstances have impaired his ability to control his temper.

Through experiments and studies, Muraven and Baumeister revealed that when a situation demands two back-to-back acts involving self-control, people tend to do worse on the second act, as they have used up their supply of self-control on the first one.

Imagine standing in a long line to get inside a restaurant. Now imagine that, once you're inside, you have to stand in another long line to get to your table. Those of us with less willpower would just get frustrated and leave.

In one of the most famous studies conducted on the subject, Baumeister gathered sixty-seven participants in a room that smelled of fresh-baked chocolate chip cookies. He divided the participants into two groups. One group was allowed to eat the cookies and the other could eat only radishes. Then, the participants were asked to complete a logic test.

Those who ate the chocolate chip cookies were able to work on the test much longer than those who ate radishes. The radish-eaters had already used up most of their self-control. As a result, they gave up after only a few minutes.

Another factor to consider is the amount of willpower we are able to tap into. Researchers have established that we each have a certain level of willpower strength that we have developed. Those who have strong willpower can more easily control their tempers, control a diet, and resist short-term distractions and temptations.

Based on this, Muraven and Baumeister made another important observation in their research that might seem pretty obvious at first glance: tasks that require more willpower will delete your supply faster than those that require less self-control.

This is why it's better to set smaller goals instead of bigger ones; so we don't become overwhelmed. Smaller goals take less willpower to accomplish.

Psychologists have also recently begun researching other factors that limit our willpower. Listed below are some of the things they've discovered in their many tests.

Sleep

One body of scientists suggests that willpower is intricately linked to physical factors such as sleep. Dr. Kelly McGonigal of Stanford University conducted a study to determine the connection between willpower and sleep deprivation.

In this study, she used severe drug addicts as test subjects to study the correlation between their sleeping patterns and drug habit relapses. One group was allowed seven hours of sleep a night while the other was allowed to sleep for eight hours each night.

The results showed that by a very strong correlation, the group that slept more was able to avoid relapses more often than the group that slept seven hours.

Dr. McGonigal concluded that the portion of the brain which is responsible for differentiating between immediate pleasures versus long term benefits gets dulled due to lack of sleep, and we end up making poorer choices due to weakened willpower.

Research shows that getting too little sleep acts like a chronic stress on the brain which makes it lose control over its cravings response functions. Under normal circumstances, the brain would be able to cope with a craving in the usual way; however, in sleep deprived circumstances, the brain would go into overdrive and create an unwarranted reaction to commonplace situations.

Glucose

Some scientists have suggested that willpower depletion may, in fact, be due to physical factors such as levels of glucose present in the body. Matthew T. Gailliot, Roy F. Baumeister, and other researchers have written a paper on the connection between self-control and glucose levels in the body. They have conducted studies and tests in the laboratory which conclusively showed three important results.

First, acts of self-control lead to a reduction of the body's blood glucose levels. Therefore, resisting the temptation to tell someone off during a heated discussion will reduce your supply of blood glucose.

Second, after one self-control task, the low level of blood glucose leads to poor performance on the next one. So after the heated discussion, a smoker might feel the urge to smoke a cigarette to relax himself.

Finally, replenishing the glucose supply after one self-control task does not show worsened performance on a subsequent self-control task. So, if he'd replenished his blood glucose supply after the heated argument, the smoker may not have needed that cigarette at all.

Religion & Beliefs

Religion and beliefs is another factor thought to influence willpower and self-control. In a study by Professor Michael McCullough of the University of Miami, it was found that religious people have more self-control than people who do not hold strong (or any) religious beliefs and that the former group may be better at achieving their long-term goals and aspirations than others.

McCullough waded through over eight decades of data collected from various fields such as economics, psychology, social sciences, and other fields.

Consistently, the religious people were less likely to abuse drugs, they performed better in school, they typically obeyed the law, and they were healthier and happier, and lived longer lives than their non-religious counterparts.

Some of the conclusions that Professor McCullough and his research team drew from their work are given below:

1) When a person indulges in religious rituals such as prayers and meditation, it directly impacts the part of the human brain most important for controlling willpower and making rational decisions.

2) When a person considers a goal to be "holy", "divine," or "sacred," he will put more effort into achieving it, and he will subsequently be more successful.

3) Religion defines standards of behavior very clearly, and the eventuality of being under observation by a higher power helps to keep a person in check. He will be more likely to keep his actions under control.

Even non-religious beliefs have been shown to have a direct impact on willpower.

In a paper published in Psychological Science, Veronika Job, Carol Dweck, and Gregory Walton showed that the degree to which a person's willpower gets depleted depends on that person's internal beliefs about his own willpower.

In this study, people were asked a number of questions about willpower, such as whether they thought that willpower was a limited or unlimited resource.

The answers were fairly evenly divided. Let's divide the limited and unlimited belief groups into group A & B respectively, for simplicity.

After answering the questions, people were given tricky tasks to perform, and their responses were judged. The results conclusively showed that people in group B (the unlimited group) performed much better on the second task, whereas group A (the limited group) made far more mistakes.

This goes to show that if a person believes that his willpower is limited, then his willpower gets depleted more quickly as opposed to a person who believes that their willpower is unlimited.

In another study, the same researchers subtly manipulated participants' beliefs about willpower by using biased questionnaires and then measured their behavior.

One type of questionnaire made people agree with statements that suggested that willpower is finite. Let's call it group C. An example of this statement would be: "A 9-5 job is mentally exhausting and one needs a break before doing something else."

The other type of questionnaire made people agree with the opposite point of view that willpower is unlimited. This one is called group D. An example of this statement would be: "Performing mentally strenuous tasks is challenging and invigorating."

After filling out these questionnaires, groups C and D performed the same activities as groups A and B before them. The results of this study showed that group C performed more poorly on task 2 as compared to group D.

This shows that because group C had been made to believe that they had limited willpower, they demonstrated a diminished amount of willpower on subsequent tasks whereas group D kept right at it because they thought they had an unlimited supply of willpower.

The results were markedly different, but the only real difference between the two groups was what they had been led to believe by the questionnaires.

Mood

Muraven, Baumeister, and their team also tried to establish a link between the effects of mood on willpower. They conducted an experiment in which they enhanced the subjects' moods by showing them funny video clips and giving them presents and observing their willpower.

By doing this, they demonstrated that people in a good mood can overcome the willpower depletion that is generally observed when two back to back tasks are performed.

Ayelet Fishbach and Aparna Labroo also conducted studies to test the effect of mood on self-control in a paper published in the Journal of Personality and Social Psychology. Their study was similar to that of Muraven and Baumeister. The data was collected from several fields but the results were consistent each time.

You've probably experienced this in your own life. Think of a time when you worked harder than usual on a project. Maybe it was for an important client at work and you really put your heart and soul into it.

You go to the presentation absolutely exhausted but well prepared. You swear when this is all over you're going to skip out early and go home and take a nap. You show the client your work and they are ecstatic. They love it!

Suddenly, you have all this energy you didn't have before. Your whole mood shifts. You leave the meeting and decide to go back to your office to tackle another project. All of a sudden, the work that seemed so draining has become your source of energy. Your mood has been changed, and your willpower has been replenished.

Stress

Stress is cited as one of the major reasons that people overeat, smoke, drink, and generally make poor decisions. According to research, when you're under stress, the part of the brain that makes conscious and rational choices gets blocked out.

Instead, the automatic response generator gets turned on. When this happens, we end up making impulsive choices that provide us with immediate gratification as opposed to long-term benefits.

For instance, an impending project deadline has us automatically reaching for an unhealthy snack because our brain gets flooded with impulses when we're stressed.

The rational part of our brain – the part that would normally come into play and warn us about the unhealthy consequences of eating the snack - would be momentarily blocked out.

Dr. Kelly McGonigal and various other researchers have dug deep into this field of study and they describe it as "flicking a switch." That is, when stress hormones are released, our impulsive side is switched on and our rational, conscious decision-making side is switched off.

So when we're in a stressful situation, our minds literally lose control. We end up making poor, thoughtless choices that we will very likely end up regretting later.

What's worse is that stress blocks our ability to foresee the consequences of a bad decision.

So, while you're stressed and you have a cigarette, or reach for an unhealthy snack, your brain fools you into believing that this act is really going to make you feel better, while stifling the warnings or alarm bells that should've gone off in your head when reaching for that snack or cigarette.

Only later, when you're stress-free, does the brain process those rational feelings of guilt and you find yourself wondering how you caved in.

Noise

Another form of stress that researchers have found affects willpower is noise—but only if the noise is unpredictable. This holds true even after exposure to the noise has ended.

For instance, in one study, one group of people was exposed to random, loud noises while the other group was not. Afterwards, both groups' performance on proofreading and other frustrating tasks were measured.

The results showed that the group initially exposed to noise did much worse on the proofreading and frustration tolerance tasks than the control group.

In the next study, two groups of participants were again selected, one exposed to noise and the other which was not. This time, however, the participants exposed to noise were given a button and told that they could press the button to terminate the noise if they wished, making the noise controllable.

After this, the participants were removed from the noisy room and the same tests as before were conducted. Interestingly enough, no one pressed the button and both groups performed equally on the proofreading and frustration tolerance tasks.

This goes to show that when people felt that the noise was controllable, it did not affect their self-control and tolerance abilities.

Crowds

Crowding has been called a potential stressor by some researchers. Just as with noise, crowds impact a person's self-control performance even after being removed from the noisy or crowded situation. And just as with the noise, people with perceived control over the situation did much better at self-control tasks than people who felt stuck in the situation.

In 1974, the Sherrod experiment tracked the performance of groups of eight female high school students performing various small tasks in crowded or less crowded rooms.

Afterwards, their persistence in solving an unsolvable puzzle was measured. The findings were the same as with the noise experiment. The group exposed to the crowd performed worse than the other group.

Similarly, in a second experiment, the group was given perceived control over the crowding option by telling them that they could move to another room while performing the first set of tasks.

Just as before, no one chose to leave the room, but having that option allowed them to perform better on their puzzles than before. In this experiment, both groups performed well.

Smell

Just as with crowds and noise, odor can also be a stressor. In the same way that people exposed to noise and crowds were tested, people were also tested when exposed to smell. The same results occurred: control helped people perform tasks better than without.

The research in all these experiments clearly shows that when you perceive yourself to be in control of a situation, you are able to tap into more willpower. But it also created a very interesting question for further research.

Why didn't any of the test groups choose to stop the noise, the crowds, or the smell? Why is giving up anything so hard – even something unpleasant?

Researchers studied this as well. What they found is that people dislike having to "give something up", even if giving it up makes them no worse off, or even better off than before. So much so, that when someone or something tries to budge them out of their usual situation, they will go out of their way to maintain the status quo.

To test this theory, the three doors game was devised by Dan Ariely, a professor of behavioral economics at M.I.T. Professor Ariely actually paid people cash rewards for playing the game, so it mimicked a real life situation as closely as possible.

The object of the game was to score rewards by clicking on doors to open them, and then clicking to claim the rewards you found inside. The people had a maximum of fifty clicks allotted to them.

The most effective strategy was to see which door had the highest reward behind it and then to continue clicking that door. Switching between doors would be costly, as clicks were wasted on opening different doors. Once you found which door had the highest reward, the best move was to just keep clicking at the prize behind it.

Professor Ariely developed two versions of the game. The first version consisted of normal play with three doors and a prize behind each door. In the modified version, a door which had not been clicked for a certain amount of time would begin to shrink and would eventually disappear.

Half of the players were asked to play the normal version first, followed by the modified version. The other half was asked to play the modified version first, followed by the normal version.

The undeniable conclusion that Professor Ariely drew from his experiment was that when people saw the doors disappearing, they panicked and immediately went to the shrinking door to retrieve it - even though they knew that that door would not bring them the highest reward!

People were willing to sacrifice their reward in order to avoid the loss of the option of the third door. In the modified, or disappearing door version, 58% of people switched doors more often as compared to the normal version, leading to a 9% reduction in overall rewards.

So people were willing to switch doors in order to keep their options open - even if those options were not beneficial for them!

This is the same tendency that drives shoppers to go crazy at sales, or packrats to collect years' worth of junk in their attics. Even though shoppers know they don't need most of the stuff they buy at sales, and people who hoard things know they don't need the junk they store in attics, they simply do not have the willpower to let go.

Shoppers lack the self-control to pass up a good bargain, and hoarders can't find it in themselves to throw out the piles of useless junk they've accumulated. People hate limiting their options, even bad ones.

As you can see, there is a lot that can affect your willpower. But there are two additional factors that we haven't touched on yet; delayed gratification and temptations. These factors can also have a huge impact on your willpower. We'll dive into them in the next chapter.

What Gets In Our Way?

Every conquering temptation represents a new fund of moral energy. Every trial endured and weathered in the right spirit makes a soul nobler and stronger than it was before.

~ *William Butler Yeats*

We've talked about the many factors that can affect willpower, but now we're going to dive deeper. We're going to go straight into the heart of what willpower represents and how it works when faced with temptation. To understand the process, we will start with delayed gratification and what research reveals about our ability to handle this kind of task.

Delayed gratification

As you recall from earlier in the book, willpower, as defined by famous researcher Roy F. Baumeister, is the adequacy of a person's strength to overcome an unwanted impulse, feeling, or thought. Linked to this definition is the concept of delayed gratification.

Delaying gratification means exactly that; it means waiting to do or obtain something rather than giving in to your impulses. Delayed gratification, then, is the "strength" referred to in Baumeister's definition of willpower.

Conversely, willpower is the ability to delay gratification of your desires. So the basic premise for delayed gratification is the same; that is, using your willpower to avoid yielding to temptation. Therefore, when a shopper resists buying a pair of must have leather boots on sale, she is using delayed gratification. And when a dieter resists a cookie, he is operating on the same principle.

The most famous and longest running experiment on the subject of delayed gratification is the marshmallow experiment conducted by Walter Mischel of Stanford University.

This experiment was conducted at the Bing Nursery School at Stanford using a number of four- to six-year olds as test subjects. The children were led to a distraction-free environment where they were given a choice of their favorite treats such as Oreo cookies, marshmallows, or pretzels.

The condition of the experiment was that the experimenter would leave the room while the treat was placed in front of the child, and the child would have to decide between consuming it now or consuming it later.

If the child chose to consume it right away, they could ring a bell and the experimenter would return; then the child could consume their chosen treat. However, if the child decided to wait fifteen minutes to consume it, they would get two of their chosen treats in return for waiting. The experimenters offered these treats to the children, and then went out of the room to observe in secret.

The results of the experiment were varied. Some children just ate the treat as soon as the researcher left the room. Some waited a little while and attempted to exercise some self-control; they sniffed the marshmallow, poked at it, played with it or attempted to distract themselves by covering their eyes, spinning around in their chairs, and trying not to think about it. But, they eventually gave in and rang the bell or just ate the candy. A few kids, however, successfully managed to wait the full fifteen minutes and were awarded the second piece of candy.

Mischel conducted this study at his daughters' school when they were about the same age as the children in the study, and the results did not seem significant to him when he originally ran the tests. It was only much later, when his daughters were in high school and he asked them about their friends' progress over the years that he realized the stark correlation between the test results and the children's overall progress in their life.

He realized that the children who had exhibited self-control during the original tests now had better grades, were healthier, in trusting relationships, and were less likely to be obese.

Dr. Mischel decided to track these individuals' progress more closely. He contacted the test subjects from the original research and got their consent to do a variety of other tests on them, including brain scans. He tracked this data periodically and the results seemed to consistently hold true.

A simple test of willpower administered when the children were between four and six was a consistent indicator of these individuals' progress in life. He even noticed that the "low delayers" seemed to have more behavioral problems, lower S.A.T. scores, and a higher crime and drug record.

For instance, a pair of siblings named Carolyn Weisz and Craig Weisz participated in the original research conducted by Dr. Mischel at Stanford. Although Carolyn was very fond of marshmallows, she was a strong-willed child and was able to hold out for the full fifteen minutes. Her brother, Craig, was among those children who immediately gobbled up their treats.

Carolyn Weisz is quoted as a textbook example of a "high delayer." She attended Stanford as an undergraduate, got her Ph.D. at Princeton, and is now an associate professor at a renowned university. Her brother, on the other hand, moved to Los Angeles, dabbled in the entertainment industry, and is currently struggling with his career in filmmaking.

This difference does not exist only in these siblings; Mischel's marshmallow test results have been replicated by many researchers over the decades since the original research was conducted in the sixties.

Another long-term study conducted in New Zealand yielded the same pattern of results. Terrie Moffitt and her team from Duke University studied and tracked data of a thousand individuals from birth to age thirty-two.

They found that people with high self-control in childhood became adults with better health and financial security, were more successful professionally, and had fewer behavioral issues and criminal records.

"Hot" and "cool" systems of the brain

Based on the results of the marshmallow experiment, Walter Mischel propounded an important theory known as the "hot and cool system" by which our minds function. His research results made him wonder exactly what the process is that leads a person to either resist or give in to temptation. More specifically, what goes through a person's mind "cognitively, emotionally, and behaviorally" when they make a conscious decision to forsake immediate gratification for the sake of a long-term benefit? The answer lies in the theory that famously came to be known as the "hot and cool mechanism" of the mind.

Mischel proposed that there are two types of processing systems in our brain; the hot system and the cool system, involving distinct characteristics and behavioral patterns.

The hot system is the emotional component of the brain; it is a simple, fast processor that acts on reflexes and impulses and is highly triggered by stress in the environment.

The cool system on the other hand, is exactly as the name suggests; cool, calm and collected. It is called the "know" system because it is the rational decision-making part of the brain, which functions reflectively and makes informed self-control decisions. The cool system is set back by stress in the environment.

Mischel suggests that the hot system develops very early in life, whereas the cool system takes time to develop. During the marshmallow experiment, children who grabbed the marshmallow and immediately gobbled it up were driven by the hot system. The children who waited and held out for the second one were driven by the cool "know" system of the brain.

We face these challenges ourselves on a daily basis when we have to decide between many tempting choices, such as sticking to a healthy eating plan versus caving in and reaching for a high calorie snack at work, or sleeping a few hours longer on a Saturday morning as opposed to waking up and getting our work done.

The development of the hot and cool systems as conscious mechanisms of the brain has evolved and now emerged into a widely accepted and acclaimed scientific viewpoint, but this has not always been the case.

Previous research in the field of willpower abandoned this premise completely by propounding the view that whatever we think, do, and feel is controlled by biological impulses in the brain and has nothing to do with conscious decision making. This theory was widely accepted in the nineteenth century as proposed by Sigmund Freud. Then, in the early twentieth century, B. F. Skinner's research proposed the exact opposite viewpoint—that decision making is entirely external and human beings' actions are shaped by external influences and stimuli in the environment.

It wasn't until Walter Mischel conducted his studies that the idea of a conscious internal thought process was put forward. He reasoned that what was important was not merely the existence of these two systems within the brain, but the interaction of these two systems with each other which led to a mix of emotional as well as cognitive behavior.

We are not always rational and we are not always emotional. In any given situation, the decision we make is usually guided by both our emotions and our logical thought processes.

There are a variety of factors which determine whether the hot or the cool system is dominant in decision making. One of the major determinants is the developmental phase of the person. The hot system is dominant during the early years of childhood and the cold system develops more as the child grows older. We can see children making more calculated decisions as they grow older. The same results were also noticed by Mischel and his colleagues in the marshmallow experiment; that older children tend to show more restraint than younger children.

The second important factor, as we've already discussed a little, is stress. The hot system is triggered by stress while the cool system can function up to a certain level under stress. But it becomes increasingly dysfunctional under increasing levels of stress.

When a person is stressed, the hot system of his brain tunes out the negative consequences of his decisions and focuses only on the perceived "reward." We have most likely faced this pressure very often in our daily lives as well. How many of us can say we haven't made a bad decision under stress? Ask anyone who's trying to watch their weight and they'll tell you countless stories about stress eating.

Stress is also the major reason college students consume so much alcohol during finals. Under normal circumstances, we know that it's counter intuitive to consume alcohol while preparing for exams. But when we're stressed, we tend to make impulsive decisions. Now we know that it's because stress triggers the hot system and outweighs the cool system, which leads us to quick, impulsive, and thoughtless decisions.

Stress not only impacts our thoughts and decisions at that moment, but if chronically present, it may even impair the ability of our cool system to operate efficiently in the long run.

Recall the example of the physical laborer working double shifts from chapter four. Because of the chronic stress he faces at work and at home, and with no social outlet, his cool system will keep suffering at the expense of the hot system and his impulsive side will tend to surface more often than the rational side.

Temptations

Whether it's high calorie snacks, an extra glass of wine at dinner, your favorite site to surf on the web, or a sale at the mall, temptations of all shapes and sizes surround us on a regular basis. We are constantly battling with ourselves to monitor our behavior in reacting to these temptations.

In one theory by Dianne M. Tice and Ellen Bratslavsky, it has been suggested that we yield to temptations in an attempt to regulate our mood. When we are in an unhappy mood, we sometimes look for comforting stimuli such as entertainment, food, alcohol, or cigarettes.

Research and studies have shown that many people say they overeat, drink, and smoke in order to feel good about themselves and that trying to stop themselves from these activities made them feel sad, anxious, and worried. We want to make better choices, but when exposed to stress, we act impulsively and break our own resolve.

Research has shown that there are two stages in the process of yielding to temptations. The first stage is the initial lapse stage. For instance, when a dieter reaches for a cookie or an ex-smoker reaches for a cigarette. This is followed by a fully escalated binge or "snowball" effect: when a person feels that, once they've broken the rules, there's no going back. They then fully indulge in whatever temptation they've given in to.

After eating the first cookie, for example, the dieter will dig into the jar and eat himself crazy. After smoking the first cigarette, the ex-smoker will light up another thinking there's no difference between one cigarette or ten since he's already caved in to the impulse of smoking.

It has also been noted through research that denying yourself what you desire may lead to a downward spiral of self-control loss. For instance, a person trying to control their spending might stop herself from buying a new outfit at the mall. This, however, will put her in a bad mood. In an effort to reduce the negative consequences of that, she may overindulge by making an unwanted or extravagant purchase, even though this would further strain her budget.

Research into consumers' buying patterns suggests that shoppers have very often been shown to sacrifice their carefully planned budgets and long-term goals when shopping. This has given rise to such sayings in popular culture as "shop till you drop," leading therapists and researchers to believe that impulsive shopping is more than just a momentary weakness.

Another common type of temptation we yield to almost every day in small measure or large is procrastination, which is the impulse to avoid or delay work. A person chooses to procrastinate for short-term gratification at the expense of achieving long-term goals.

For instance, a student may have school deadlines in the near future but may keep putting it off for whatever reason. When the deadline creeps up and the procrastinating student panics and sets to work, not only is she likely to do a worse job at the last minute, but she will also feel more stressed and overworked than if she had been working diligently throughout the project.

Delayed gratification and temptations play an important role in understanding willpower and how our brains work.

Now that we have all the pieces to what constitutes willpower and what affects it, it's time to put it all together and see what willpower looks like in action. In the next chapter, we'll go over the four broad categories of willpower and the way they are interconnected.

How Do Our Thoughts and Emotions Affect Our Willpower?

It is not the critic who counts; not the man who points out how the strong man stumbles, or where the doer of deeds could have done them better. The credit belongs to the man who is actually in the arena, whose face is marred by dust and sweat and blood, who strives valiantly; who errs and comes short again and again; because there is not effort without error and shortcomings; but who does actually strive to do the deed; who knows the great enthusiasm, the great devotion, who spends himself in a worthy cause, who at the best knows in the end the triumph of high achievement and who at the worst, if he fails, at least he fails while daring greatly. So that his place shall never be with those cold and timid souls who know neither victory nor defeat.

~Theodore Roosevelt

Now it's time to take what we know about willpower and put it all together. We already know that willpower stems from our energy to control our actions, avoid temptations, and be productive. But now we're going to look at how it works in relation to the other systems in our brain.

We are going to look at the four broad categories of willpower.

Thoughts

The first category of willpower is thoughts. Have you ever heard the little joke, "Don't think about an elephant. You just thought about an elephant, didn't you?" Have you ever been working on something that you just can't focus on? For instance, if you're at work trying to finish a difficult project, but you also have a sick child at home, it can be hard to focus on work when thoughts of your child keep creeping into your head.

Both work and your child are important, but you have to learn to prioritize and focus on the work in front of you.

That's what this category of willpower controls. We use willpower to focus on what we need to focus on while keeping all other thoughts at bay. This isn't always an easy thing to do, but, with practice, you can start to learn how to focus on one thing at a time.

Emotions

The second category of willpower is emotions. Our self-control isn't at our best when we don't feel at our best. If we come down with a cold, all our energy will be focused on getting well. We will have none left over for accessing our willpower.

This applies to our emotions as well. If we're feeling down, it can be hard to muster up the will to work on anything. For example, many people suffer from seasonal depression. If winter lasts longer than usual, it can be hard to get yourself off the couch and do something productive. It's cold and gray outside, and all you want to do is curl up on the couch with a blanket and a cup of hot cocoa.

Emotions can drain your willpower, too. Just like using your self-control all day long can make you feel drained by the end of the day, manipulating your emotions for an entire day can also drain you of your willpower.

For example, you might have a close friend who's had a rough day, so you try to pretend to be in a better mood than you are to help her feel better. Putting up this fake emotional front can drain you physically and emotionally just as other uses of your willpower can exhaust you. Always be aware of your thoughts and emotions to practice using them in a constructive way.

Impulses

The third category of willpower is impulses. Think back to the last time you forced yourself to go on a diet. It takes a lot of hard work and focus. And, as we all know, that first slip-up on the diet usually means the end of the diet. The most common thing that kills a diet is an impulse.

This is where all of the categories start to pile together. When you diet, you might get a sudden impulse to eat some chips. You can call it an impulse or a craving, but either way, it's almost impossible to ignore until we satiate that impulse. And then, it's hard to stop that impulse from snowballing.

Unlike our thoughts or emotions, impulses are harder to control because they are often thoughts that pop into our heads. While you can minimize the types of impulses you give into by taking preventative measures, such as removing all chips from your house, you don't have control over whether or not you still think about the chips.

That's where willpower comes in. Willpower can help how you act on this impulse and whether or not you choose to ignore it or act upon it. For instance, you could change your impulse by saying something like, "I want chips. That means I want something crunchy. I'm going to eat some carrots."

Or, you could redirect your chain of thoughts completely. You could say something like, "I'm going to do a crossword puzzle or play Words with Friends instead of eating chips." Willpower can help you weigh the consequences of ignoring or giving in to your impulses, cravings, or temptations by helping you reason with yourself.

Performance Control

The final category of willpower is performance control. This final category combines the first three categories together and applies that to itself. Performance Control lets you know how well you can focus on a job. It deals with how long you can focus on a task without giving up, how much effort or willpower it takes to complete a task, and whether or not you procrastinate or manage your time well.

Think back to the paper you procrastinated on from Chapter Two. You had good intentions to finish the paper. You might have even opened a book or two and gotten out some paper. Maybe you wrote a sentence or two. But you never got further than that on your project. This was your chance to control your performance. Willpower is the thing that could have helped you focus more and procrastinate less.

Procrastination is willpower's biggest enemy. It's easy to put off work and put off work because "there's still time." Then, when the date gets closer, it's even harder to finish the task at hand. Have you ever had the feeling that you have too much to do in such a short amount of time, so you just don't start at all? You might think to yourself, "Well, I'm not going to be able to finish it in time anyway, so I might as well not do it at all."

All of this negativity adds up and is right there when you're ready to work on your next project. You think to yourself, "Well, I couldn't do the last one, so why would I be able to do this one?" You might pick something easier or abandon the project altogether.

Each of the four categories of willpower contributes to how we think about what we need to do from project to project. It's all connected. Remember, researchers believe that willpower is a finite resource. The reason why all of it is connected is because we don't have a supply of willpower lined up for each category—it all comes from the same source.

If you spend all of your time pushing off negative thoughts and emotions, you might not have anything left to dispel impulses or cravings you might have. And when it comes time to finally focus on the project, you won't have any self-control left to get it done.

So how can we find a balance between these four categories in order to use our willpower wisely and accomplish more with less stress?

We set goals. We'll dive into the goal-setting process in the following chapter, as well as the most common mistakes that can kill your chances of success.

What Is the Secret to Strengthening Our Willpower?

Good and evil both increase at compound interest. That is why the little decisions you and I make every day are of such infinite importance. The smallest good act today is the capture of a strategic point from which, a few months later, you may be able to go on to victories you never dreamed of. An apparently trivial indulgence in lust or anger today is the loss of a ridge or railway line or bridgehead from which the enemy may launch an attack otherwise impossible.

~ C.S. Lewis

Before we get into goal setting, we need to lay out what researchers have discovered about strengthening one's self-control. It's important to understand the reasoning behind a certain course of action so you can fully embrace the process.

Fortunately, there has been substantial research done in this area. So let's dive in and see what we can do to strengthen our willpower.

Out of Sight – Out of Mind

One effective tactic for improving our self-control is avoiding temptation. If sweets are your willpower challenge, then keep away from situations where you will be tempted. If alcohol is difficult for you to resist, then steer clear of events where alcohol may be your only beverage option. If you tend to get lost on Pinterest, then disable your Internet while working on a project. The act of avoiding temptation altogether is mainly using the "out of sight, out of mind" approach. You make yourself believe that if you don't see it, then it doesn't exist.

Think back to the marshmallow experiment. The researcher told the children that they could have just one marshmallow if they didn't want to wait. However, if they waited a few minutes, he would reward them with two marshmallows.

Some children sat and stared at the marshmallows. They sat starting at them hoping for time to pass quickly and receive their second marshmallow. Other children looked away or closed their eyes during the waiting period. They distracted themselves so they wouldn't think about what they were passing up.

Interestingly enough, it was these children who distracted themselves that had the greatest amount of success in receiving the later (double marshmallow) reward. Those who sat and stared at the single marshmallow had greater instances of just giving in and eating the one. Sitting and staring at their temptation proved to be too difficult. But those children who practiced (in their own way) the out of sight, out of mind strategy, had a greater chance of success.

This works in a simple way for adults too. In another study it was found that adults who kept candy or sweets in their desk at work were less likely to indulge in them than those who had the same sweets and treats sitting out in view on their desks. The power of suggestion was too much of a drain on their willpower; but if they didn't see the candy, they were less likely to indulge. When kept in the drawer, it was out of sight and out of mind.

Implementation Intention & Planning Ahead of Time

Another effective tactic for improving self-control is something referred to as implementation intention. It is more commonly known as an "if this, then that" approach. If you do this, then you get that.

This step to improving willpower requires a little pre-planning. People plan ahead rather than having to rely on their willpower in that moment. So if you have a hard time resisting an extra glass of wine at dinner, then you plan ahead and say to yourself, "If someone asks me if I'd like an alcoholic drink, then I'll ask for a club soda instead".

Basically you prepare yourself to deal with temptation in advance. Similarly, diabetic people or someone with a weakness towards sweets should plan ahead and use this willpower tactic when going out to eat or to attend a function where they are not aware what will food will be served. If someone asks them if they would like dessert, they will counter attack the temptation by asking for sorbet or fresh fruit instead.

If there is a long buffet table at social gatherings, then a healthier choice is to possibly take a smaller plate or take larger portions of items that are healthier. This leaves less room on the plate for those items that you need to refrain from eating (high calorie, sweets etc.).

When tackling surfing the net, you could use a similar approach. If I want to surf rather than work, then I will take a five minute break after 20 minutes of concentrated work.

Practicing the "if this - then that" approach helps people by saving them from having to make a split second decision. It will help build up willpower to use when, in the face of temptation, your willpower may not be the strongest.

This is supported by a vast amount of research and studies discussed in previous chapters about the likeness of willpower to our body's muscles. Just as our own physical muscles get weak and need strengthening, so do our willpower and self-control "muscles". When not exercised, they can grow weak as well.

This same premise has been seen to be effective with those attempting to go to the gym and begin a workout routine as well. I think we've all been there. We have good intentions – the best of intentions actually - but somewhere along the way we slip.

We start out strong. We go purchase new tennis shoes to wear to the gym and even purchase new workout clothes and get all ready to get moving. We're great the first few times, and then our willpower wanes a bit. We miss a day, and then we miss maybe two. And before you know it those new tennis shoes and new workout clothes are collecting dust.

On the other hand sticking with the goal - even on days when it seems extremely taxing to get up and go to the gym - will eventually lead to a new habit. The most important thing to remember is to set clear goals for yourself, practice hard to get there, and then stick to the goal (through good times and often not so good times).

This is shown to help develop your self-control and willpower muscles. By strengthening these muscles, you will be able to stay strong when faced with temptation.

This strategy has also been recommended by Margaret Moore, who is the founder and chief executive officer of Well Coaches Corporation. Margaret advocates and coaches her clients about how to plan in advance in order to conserve your willpower.

She says that the lowest level of self-control we face is when we're hungry and tired, and that is the worst time to make any decisions. This concept has also been given attention in many scientific studies regarding willpower which show that making any sort of choices leads to ego depletion, or loss of self-control.

Margaret Moore's suggestion is to plan and organize various aspects of your life in such a way that you don't have to think and decide all the time. For instance, there ought to be no 'decision" about going to the gym or about what to eat. You should have pre decided certain days of the week where you will meet up with a gym buddy, and you will have your meals planned in advance so you don't get tempted to eat something unhealthy when you come home from work hungry and tired.

She advocates making healthy choices well in advance when your willpower level is high; this way you have to make "no choice" when you actually have to implement the decision.

This is another reason why so many time management experts advocate to do lists or some variation of the concept. When you have a predetermined set of items to do for the day, you don't have to exert willpower to decide what actions to take.

You should also plan ahead in order to proactively deal with obstacles. We all face mental hurdles and barriers when trying to achieve something. The key is to identify and get rid of these barriers before they hamper us.

This has been researched by Dr. Falko F. Sniehotta and his team. Dr. Sniehotta is the president of the European Health Psychology Society and is also the Associate Editor of Health Psychology Review. He believes that planning is the most valuable tool in the process of changing unhealthy behavior as it overcomes the gap between intentions and actual behavior.

His study concluded that those people who wrote their goals and plans in a journal were better equipped to deal with hurdles. They were also more likely to stick with an exercise regime as compared to those who made no such plans.

A second study conducted by Webb & Sheeran found that making goals and plans helped people to succeed at difficult tasks requiring self-control, even after they had used up their willpower in a previous task. In other words, creating goals and plans helped replenish their supply of willpower.

A similar concept explored by Baumeister and Bushman is the Zeigarnik effect. It is formally defined as "the tendency to experience intrusive thoughts about an objective that was once pursued and left incomplete."

The theory basically states that unfinished tasks and goals tend to stay in our conscious mind, but once the goal is accomplished, these reminders stop interrupting us.

Therefore, if a student has an unfinished college paper to submit, she may be pelted with reminders from her brain even though she is not consciously trying to think about it.

Even more interesting than the original idea of the Zeigarnik effect is the subsequent discovery that the "reminders" don't necessarily stop only when we accomplish something – it may also be sufficient to just make plans to accomplish it.

This concept was explored in an experiment where students were asked to first think actively about an important exam. Then, half of the students were told to schedule study times for the exam. The rest of the students made no plans at all. After this, all students participated in a word association test.

It was observed that those students who did not devise any plans created study-related word associations, because they had been unable to get the exam out of their heads. The other half did not have study-related word associations, because they had made concrete plans and moved on.

Just the simple act of setting goals frees your mind, and your willpower, to focus on other tasks.

The implications for this in our personal lives are tremendous. If we want to succeed at difficult tasks, then research suggests that half our effort can be saved just by planning ahead.

For someone trying to lose weight, this means making an exercise schedule, listing down the difficulties they might face and creating an action plan to overcome those hurdles.

Similarly, if you've been trying to create good reading habits in yourself, it will help to make a list of books you might be interested in and determining a specific time for reading.

If you're looking to start a business it's important that you determine the actions you need to take, and break those down into daily achievable steps.

Aimee Kimball, a sports mental health trainer states that planning is one of the most important aspects of starting and sticking with an exercise program. She asks people to identify and list down what they feel is hampering their progress and then to visualize themselves attaining success.

Planning and setting up default "if this, then that" responses can be applied to any kind of task or challenge requiring willpower. Once a person has already decided what to do and how to respond when faced with temptation, then this becomes their reflex response. They don't have to think about what to do in a difficult situation. The default response is automatically triggered when faced with the temptation and it becomes much easier to implement the pre-planned strategy.

For example, one might decide in advance that every time you are tempted to smoke, you will take 10 deep breaths and have a glass of water instead. Then when you get the craving, your body uses the default or pre-planned signal to have water and breathe deeply.

Goal Setting

As you can see, planning ahead is crucial. This is where goals come in. We have already briefly discussed the importance of setting goals to achieve what we wish to accomplish. Now that you have a deeper understanding of how willpower works, you can understand why goal setting is so important.

Setting small, attainable goals helps you preserve your willpower and leads to less procrastination. Goals are easily tracked, which allows you to monitor your progress. Realizing your progress toward a goal will motivate you and strengthen your willpower in the future. Goal setting is a very powerful way to increase your success – provided you create suitable goals.

When goals are set properly, they act as a positive and powerful motivator, providing you with added vision and enthusiasm. However, poor goal setting has the opposite effect. It can hamper your progress and lead to frustration, anger, and cause lackluster effort.

Think about the last work or school project that went wrong. The typical pattern in failed goal setting tasks is that everything starts out well and you initially make progress.

However, when something goes wrong, everything starts to unravel. The goal either takes longer to complete than you initially thought or you end up becoming discouraged due to unforeseen obstacles that arise. Before you know it, the goal is forgotten and the project starts to suffer.

To help stop this unproductive cycle, it's crucial that you know the reasons why goal setting most often goes awry.

Here are the eight most common problems that crop up in goal setting.

Setting Unrealistic Goals

One of the most common mistakes in goal setting is setting unrealistic goals. During the goal-setting process, it's okay to dream big and let your imagination loose. But once you've actually decided on a goal, it is imperative that the goal is realistic and achievable.

For instance, if your goal is to lose weight through a controlled diet and exercise, you can't expect to lose 25 pounds in a month.

Or, if your goal is to create a profitable business, you can't expect to be a millionaire within the first six months.

Management gurus and self-help professionals advocate the use of "SMART" goal setting strategies; that is, making sure that your goals are Specific, Measurable, Attainable, Relevant, and Time bound.

Not Having Well Rounded Goals

Another common mistake in setting goals is focusing only on very limited areas of your life. When you set your goals, it's necessary to ensure that you strike the proper balance between different areas of your life. Focusing only on your career or only on your personal life will increase the likelihood that one or both of those areas will suffer. When that happens, your overall well-being will be affected.

For instance, committing to good time management, applying for a promotion, and reading one leadership book each month are all good and achievable goals, but they focus only on your professional life. Personal goals are just as important as professional ones, and achieving one will automatically boost your efforts toward achieving the other.

Underestimating Time Commitments

A third hurdle in setting goals is underestimating timelines. We can all relate to this. In fact, a study was conducted on college students asking them to list the approximate times when they would be able to hand in their research assignments. The overwhelming majority surpassed the submission deadline by more than a week, even though they were the ones who set the date.

If completion time is underestimated, it can be discouraging when the results take longer to achieve, which causes lack of motivation and skyrocketing failure rates. It is essential to schedule your goals and projects realistically, rather than outrageously.

One should also account for setbacks and delays and build them into the original timeline. For instance, a dieter who plans to lose two to three pounds per week should also be aware that there will be off days when she will cheat, or days when she might not go to the gym. A person looking to finish a novel will inevitably have days where no writing takes place. Remember, keeping realistic timelines is more likely to result in goal accomplishment.

Not Learning From Mistakes

Another goal-setting mistake involves not learning from past mistakes. Whether they're small mistakes or critical ones, we've all been there at some point. Mistakes can be costly, embarrassing, and time consuming, but they also be tremendously rewarding.

Learning from mistakes rather than dwelling on them, and keeping them in mind the next time you set goals, will ensure that you will excel where before you might have come up short.

Not Reviewing Your Progress

Accomplishing goals can also be hindered when your progress has not been reviewed thoroughly and periodically. It takes time to accomplish goals. Sometimes you may feel stuck in a certain situation or feel that your progress has tapered down. You need to analyze what to do to continue to move forward. Self-monitoring is vital to any kind of resolution. If you realize you aren't moving in the right direction, simply back up and redirect your efforts.

This is another reason why smaller goals are so much more powerful than larger ones. They allow you to determine if there is a problem or you are veering off course very quickly. They also allow you to see your success build and help strengthen your willpower "muscle".

Not Focusing On Your Victories

Another crucial step in the goal process is to celebrate your wins along the way. Most of us tend to discount our success and immediately start looking ahead to the next step. We discount all our hard work and effort that went into achieving the current milestone. It's vital that we STOP – and take time to embrace our hard work. This will not only increase your confidence level and motivation, it will help strengthen your belief in your willpower. If you have accomplished a certain phase of a goal, it's critical that you give yourself credit and celebrate your success.

Making Unappealing Goals

Another stumbling block happens when we fail to define our goals in a motivating manner. Rather than positive goals we can look forward to, we set up "negative" goals that focus on the very things we're trying to avoid. How a person perceives their goal can have a dramatic effect on their success rate.

For instance, "losing weight" has a negative connotation – it implies that you are fat and out of shape. "Getting in shape" is the same goal, rephrased in a positive way to state the same thing – that you want to get healthy.

Another example of a negative goal is to "stop working overtime," which could be rephrased in a positive way as 'to spend more time with family." Although these changes are minute and subtle, they impact the way we perceive our tasks. Negative goals are emotionally unappealing, which makes it harder for us to want to work for them.

Remember, mood is a stressor that limits willpower.

Setting Too Many Goals

The biggest and most common mistake in the goal setting process is setting too many goals. Once we start planning and setting goals, we get excited about changing our life for the better, and we start setting goals in all directions. This is why New Year's resolutions often tend to fail.

The problem is that we have a limited amount of time and energy. If we have too many goals to accomplish, then none of the goals get the attention they need to be completed successfully.

We expect too many things from ourselves all at one time, and our willpower system gets overloaded. The stress puts a strain on the amount of willpower we have. When we can't fulfill any of them, we tend to get frustrated and abandon our goals.

Research shows that by the end of January, about one third of those who set New Year's resolutions have abandoned them, and by the time it's July, more than half have derailed.

Think about your New Year's resolutions. How many did you set this year? How many are you still working on? Since we only have a single "bucket" of willpower, it makes more sense to focus on only a few goals at a time. Trying to fulfill several important goals at once will decrease your focus on each of them and diminish your chances of success.

Focus on quality rather than quantity. If you recall, another goal setting mistake is being too narrow with your goal setting. You want to strike the perfect balance. We'll go into this in more detail later in the book but a good rule of thumb is to choose one personal and one business goal and focus on those first. Work out which goals are most important at the moment, then focus on an action plan to accomplish those 2 specific goals.

Goal Setting in Action

Now that we know the mistakes to avoid, let's briefly recap the three parts that are necessary to achieving our goals. The first part is to set a goal and establish the motivation for successfully completing the goal. Second, track your progress. Keep a chart and mark your progression in reaching your goal. The final ingredient for reaching goals is willpower. No matter what the goal is, willpower and self-control are essential to achieving the outcome.

Now let's walk through the process of setting a goal to see how it works. Think about your house for a moment. Is there a room with an overabundance of clutter? Let's set a goal to get rid of the mess.

Your goal is now set: clean the room.

Display this goal prominently where you will see it every day, along with what you will gain by having the room clean. For instance, it may be because you feel so much more productive in a clean room.

Next, give yourself a time frame for accomplishing the goal. Let's make it one week. That doesn't sound too hard, does it? One week to clean a room is possible.

Now, set smaller goals for yourself. Let's say the room is your office. Start by removing any trash or things you don't need from the room. Next, decide what you need to keep and organize it. Then, choose a day to vacuum and dust the room from top to bottom. Keep making small, daily goals like this and suddenly, cleaning the room will seem easy rather than overwhelming.

Reward yourself by tracking your progress. Make a calendar and a list, and mark off each task as you achieve what you set out to complete. There's nothing quite as satisfying as crossing off an item on your to do list.

Resist the urge to put off a day's task for the next day. That's how tasks add up and cause you to feel overwhelmed. Make sure you complete each task on the day specified. Make them easy tasks that won't take too long. At the end of it, you will have completed a large job on your own without exhausting too much of your willpower.

This is the goal setting process in action.

Turbo Charge Your Goal Setting Efforts

We all value and respect the opinions of others and want people to have a good opinion of us. This can be turned into a strategy to motivate yourself; if you're having trouble sticking to your goals, then publicly share your goals with others.

Some researchers suggest sharing your goals with your closest friends, mostly through social networks like Twitter and Facebook. Some researchers even suggest sharing your goals with people outside your own network.

The website stickk.com started by two Yale University professors, Dean Karlan and Ian Ayres, uses this idea to help people achieve their goals. This internet company enables people to make online commitment "contracts" with others. Users have to agree to achieve their desired goal; these are often personal goals such as losing weight, getting into shape, quitting smoking or drinking less. Then they have to sign a legally binding contract to make a certain amount of payment if they do not achieve their goals.

This payment can be made to other individuals (people who are referred to as "Friends or Foes") or to charities. If the user selects "charity" then the recipient is selected by stickk.com itself. Users can even select "anti-charities" - that is those whose cause you do not support, as a means of motivating yourself.

A growing body of researchers suggests that making other people aware of the details of your goals will motivate you to achieve them because the threat of public humiliation is likely to keep you in check.

The other great advantage of letting someone know is that you can get valuable feedback throughout the process. Some people recommend a three step process to help achieve your goals.

1) Communicate your goals to those you trust:

Once you let others know, you can get feedback, suggestions and ideas from others and communicate your chosen deadline to everyone. Make sure you choose people who will encourage rather than discourage or sabotage your efforts.

2) Keep your social networking buddies in the loop:

After letting your trusted circle know, keep them informed of your progress. You should not make too big a deal out of it but at least keep them in the loop – even when you have setbacks. Most likely, they will empathize and support you in getting back on track.

3) Go public:

Sometimes, talking to strangers might give a fresh outlook on what you're doing and help you go about it in a better way. This will also help when your goals are uncommon and not shared by those within your inner circle.

This is made much easier with technology. For instance, an application called "MySomeday" is specifically designed to share goals with people in your community and to get constructive feedback from others. The method is to share your plan, and then others comment and provide their feedback.

A related concept here is partnering. If you find someone who is trying to accomplish the same goal as you, then pair up so you can keep each other accountable. It will become much easier to stay on track with your goal. This could be a gym buddy, your spouse, or even someone you meet online.

Just by having someone to share your ideas and troubles with, and being held accountable for your efforts, you will be much less likely to blow off your goals. You've made a commitment - and you don't want to lose credibility in the eyes of others.

The more you set goals and accomplish them, the more you are using your willpower and strengthening your willpower instinct. You are also creating powerful habits that will propel you forward. Creating habits is absolutely crucial! Once it's a habit, you don't have to use as much willpower to make it happen. This allows you to use your reserve of willpower to tackle bigger challenges.

This is the true secret to really creating momentum and change in your life.

Everything that we have learned about willpower shows that creating new habits is the real key to using our willpower in the most efficient and effective way possible.

This process is so vital that we'll spend the rest of the book showing you, step by step, exactly how to turn your actions into habits and create lasting change in your life.

How Can We Create Powerful Habits?

I am, indeed, a king, because I know how to rule myself.

~ Pietro Aretino

To say that we are "creatures of habit" is an accurate definition of human beings. All of your current circumstances are the consequences of your habits. Your physical body and health is a consequence of your individual habits. The quality of your relationships with others is a consequence of your habits. Your career and income level is a consequence of your habits.

If you are content with these aspects of your life, then your current habits are serving you well. But if there are any areas in your life you would like to improve, it's your habits that stand in your way.

Habit change is a skill and a challenge. Sometimes, what we need to pair with willpower is a little bit of strategy. So we're going to talk about ways to strategize your goals to maximize your willpower and the effects it can have on your life. After we're done, there will be no more gym cancellations by the end of January.

The first principle in breaking any habit is the "Keep It Simple Stupid" or KISS principle. Our brains like easy stuff. It's not because your brain is lazy—it just naturally fears failure. And if something seems simple, your brain is much more likely to do it. So to simplify habit change, we first need a good understanding of how your brain works.

Trying to break any habit without understanding how your brain works makes success nearly impossible. You'll easily blame yourself for your habits and see them as "your habits."

This common internalization of one's behaviors gives the habit enormous power over what a person does because the person "sees" the behavior as "them," or who they are. It can be hard to change a habit if you believe that's who you are. So there's a conflict between the habits that are you and the "you" you want to become.

Try to think of yourself as having two brains. Your conscious brain is You. It's the activity of your conscious thinking, or your Will. Your other brain is your subconscious brain, which works like a computer, running thousands of programs in your life from your heartbeat to your digestion. It also helps you assign meaning to things in the world from your experiences stored in your memory.

Your subconscious brain can be programmed to perform a remarkable range of tasks. Nearly anything you program it to do, it will do. Your subconscious brain does not have a choice—it just automatically follows the programming it was given by others or gave itself from what you experienced.

Your subconscious brain's number one job is to avoid danger to ensure your existence and survival. Just like your heart's job is to circulate blood, the organ called your brain has the job to keep you alive and out of danger.

Our ancestors would have died out long ago from taking dangerous and foolish risks without this section of the brain. Your brain mainly uses the emotion of "fear" to compel you to avoid driving 100 mph in a snowstorm, walking on a slippery roof, or giving a loaded gun to a child. This powerful brain function also compels us away from emotional danger or discomfort, like the fear of giving a speech or being criticized. Think of this as a "discomfort avoidance mechanism."

Your subconscious brain has a second default setting that compels it toward doing things that produce the feeling of pleasure and happiness. A strong inner drive toward pleasure assures we are driven to find food to live and to procreate.

If you find pleasure in drinking coffee while reading the paper in the morning, it will easily become a habit. If you enjoy eating popcorn while watching your favorite TV show in the evenings, it will easily become a habit.

Once you associate pleasure with doing something, trying to stop doing it means you'll create the discomfort of losing that source of pleasure. Your brain must avoid discomfort, so it will convince you to avoid breaking habits in order to continue feeling pleasure.

Whenever you have a thought, your brain automatically compares it to the millions of mental filing cabinets filled with every thought, idea, and belief you have stored. Based on what it finds, it will send you a signal instructing you how to feel about it and what you should do. This happens faster than snapping your finger.

The more your brain believes about something, the more it will accept ideas similar to those beliefs and reject those that are not. The more you think about anything in a certain way, the more your brain will believe and instruct you that that is how it really is and how it should be.

It does this because opposing knowledge creates discomfort from the potential of being "wrong." And remember, your brain hates discomfort. Furthermore, your brain wants to make order and sense of what you experience to make your life easier and safer—why change and risk pain or injury?

This powerful, natural way your brain works explains why habits are hard to break and why it's so "easy" to keep doing things the same way.

Now that we know a little more about the brain, let's talk about habits. A habit is a pattern of thinking and acting that has been repeated and reinforced enough times that it now happens automatically without much thought. A habit is just an association between an event or thing that triggers a meaning of what to do that is recorded in your subconscious. A habit is what your brain has learned to avoid discomfort and be comfortable.

A red traffic light is associated in your brain with a certain action to avoid danger. For some, the event of coming home from work triggers a subconscious feeling that they should eat chips to get out of the uncomfortable feeling of hunger and experience pleasure from enjoying the salty food.

When it's time for bed, it means by automatic subconscious association that it's time to brush your teeth to avoid the emotional pain of ugly teeth or the pain of the dentist chair.

A habit grows more powerful each time it is reinforced positively— meaning the action taken provides a payoff from a feeling of pleasure or the relief or avoidance of discomfort or pain. The process looks like this:

Event → Means (produces a feeling) → Learned Response → Positive Reinforcement
• Red Light → programmed to mean "stop the car or get a ticket or possibly get in an accident" → stop car → Feel good about not smashing your car or hurting others and following the law
• Morning drive to work → programmed to mean "time to drink coffee" → Drink coffee on the way to work → Enjoy the coffee
• Arrive at home after work → programmed to mean "time to eat snacks" → Eat snacks after work → Enjoy the snacks
• Watching TV after dinner → programmed to mean "time to eat popcorn" → Eat popcorn while watching TV → Enjoy the popcorn
• No cookies in house → programmed to mean "I need to make some cookies to be a good mother and spouse" → Bake cookies → Enjoy feeling like a good mother and spouse and enjoy eating a few cookies
• Feeling anxious or worried → programmed to mean "I can bite my nails to feel comfort" Bite nails → Feel comfort from biting nails
• Feeling criticized → programmed to mean "I can feel relief by criticizing back" Criticize back → Feel better

This is how your brain works. A thought is associated with a feeling of pleasure or pain that compels you either toward the pleasure or away from the pain. Once you understand this, you no longer judgmentally see what you do as "your fault," but rather what your brain compels you to do through the powerful default function to seek pleasure and avoid pain.

Understanding this allows you to take the next step—using this knowledge to create a strategy for successfully changing the habits that stand between you and what you want.

To really understand this important process, stop reading now and think about something you just recently did by habit. See each step of the sequence between your thought and what you did. Write down each step to really improve your insight and understanding.

What event or thing happened that triggered you? What meaning did your brain attach to it? What did you do? What positive reinforcement did you receive from your action?

 Once you walk yourself through this process, you no longer see what you do as "your fault"

With an understanding of how your brain works, you can see that in doing its job of keeping you out of danger and moving you toward pleasure, your brain has developed a lot of ways to do that automatically.

Many of your core habits were developed through emulation of influential adults in your life when you were just a kid, unable to choose what you really wanted or understand how those choices would later affect you. Other habits developed as responses to life's challenges and stress over the years. Your current habits have nothing to do with who you are or what you can accomplish—they do not define your ability or potential anymore than does your hair color or your height.

The habits that make you feel like doing or not doing things are the natural production of what your subconscious brain was designed to do. Knowing that your brain's habits are not your habits, frees you to identify and change them more easily than if you think they are some fixed part of who you are.

Here are a few examples of feelings your subconscious brain kicks out that may not be in your best interest. Identify what the brain is trying to do: avoid discomfort or have pleasure?

"I don't feel I should apply for that new position."

"I feel like calling her up and telling her what I really think!"

"I feel like having sweets when I drink coffee."

"I feel like popcorn when I watch TV."

"I don't feel like working on my big work project."

"I feel like talking about the people at work that drive me crazy."

""I feel like staying in bed."

"I feel like watching a movie rather than doing the bills."

When you see your brain's programming as your habits, you easily blame yourself and see your habits as your fault. This, in turn, lowers your self-confidence and puts you in a defeated state of mind which makes working past them nearly impossible.

Once you understand and believe in the separateness of YOU and your brain's functioning, you are FREE to change your programming because you don't see it as some fixed part of your personality.

You can blame your brain for your habits and stop blaming yourself, keeping you feeling good about YOU. This makes all the difference in the world when it comes to changing habits. Habits lose their power when you feel good about yourself.

Even knowing all of this, habits are still hard to break. The associated pleasure or pain avoidance you get from your habits gives them their power.

Other factors, like your body being physiologically hooked on carbohydrates, nicotine, or drugs, influence the power of the habit. However, habits like feeling compelled to stay in bed rather than go to the gym, or feeling compelled to eat a second helping, are primarily powered by your thoughts. Remember, your mind rules your body. Any physical issue is ultimately controlled by your subconscious brain.

Breaking a habit is hard because of how your subconscious brain works. It only follows directions and knows if the direction is getting the desired result. If eating cookies with your coffee has been giving you pleasure for the last three years, your brain only understands that association and cannot understand a better alternative until it experiences that alternative long enough for it to become the new habit.

Your subconscious brain knows the best way to get the result and it will pursue it automatically. Even when you introduce an alternative, it will go back to the old habit if the alternative has not established an equally strong feeling of pleasure or pain avoidance.

For example, if you have been eating a certain cookie with your coffee and you start eating a cookie that tastes better, your old habit will die. If you start eating a sugar-free cookie that gives you less pleasure, it will take willpower to keep eating the lesser cookie until the memory of the pleasure of the old cookie fades away.

Another factor that makes habit change challenging is your subconscious brain's strong tendency to avoid change. Why? Because anything that is unknown has the potential for pain; from either the potential of something going wrong or the process of needing to learn something new.

Your brain will spring into action to compel you toward solutions to get out of feeling uncomfortable. The easiest and most common way is to avoid it. So any change that causes an unknown in your life is seen as "discomfort" so your brain will produce the feeling of fear to motivate you to avoid the change so as to get back to feeling comfortable.

There are some methods to help us along the way to help develop new, better habits. For instance, what we say holds a lot of meaning. If someone says that a cookie was "very tasty" or it was "to die for," each carries a different meaning and feeling. The same goes for the word "habit." In today's society, "habit" is a bad word. It defines who we are and whether or not we're capable of handling daily tasks.

An alternative word that more accurately defines what we are talking about is a "program." When you say, "I have a program to quit smoking," it sounds more like a plan than an unattainable goal or habit. It also defines a habit as what it really is—a program of the brain that was learned, but can be unlearned.

From now on, we will refer to a "habit" as a "program." You may think "what is the big deal with what word I use?" But this is how your brain works. You use words to establish meaning to every event you experience throughout the day, and these meanings program your subconscious brain.

You are constantly programming your subconscious brain all day long with your own internally spoken self-talk, either silently in your thoughts, or in what you say out loud to yourself and others. Just by making the simple change in calling your habits "programs," you change their meaning and thus loosen their hold on you by knowing what they truly are and how they can change!

Powerful Step-by-Step Process to Change Your Life

Nobody can give you freedom. Nobody can give you equality or justice or anything. If you're a man, you take it.

~Malcolm X, Malcolm X Speaks: Selected Speeches and Statements

Step 1 - Stop Running Your Old Program

This is the obvious first step in changing a program. A person wants to stop drinking pop at work, so they decide to stop and endure the "feel like" feelings the subconscious brain pours out to get back to its comfortable program of drinking pop. A person wants to stop eating before bed, so they resolve to stop eating before bed, thus enduring the strong urge to eat when bedtime rolls around.

Over time, without the positive reinforcement, the program slowly loses its power to compel you. This is the old willpower/cold turkey/tough-it-out method of change.

However, without anything positive to replace it, or anything negative to chase the program away, it may take several months for this to happen.

This can be done.

There are people that have been successful at this brute willpower method of change. However, most people can't endure the brain's thoughts compelling them back long enough for this method alone to be successful.

Because of the tremendous energy required, the cold-turkey method can only be successful when you focus on just a single habit at a time. Even then, it's a long, hard haul to make it work. Trying to use the method with more than one habit at the same time almost always results in failure.

This is what happens with most weight loss attempts—the person tries to change several eating habits, exercise habits, schedule habits, sleep habits and more! Perhaps a dozen or more habits simultaneously—nearly impossible using the willpower-only method. It becomes completely overwhelming (a strong feeling of discomfort) and thus the brain seeks to get out of that discomfort by constantly compelling the person back toward their old programs that provide comfort so easily!

Furthermore, when you understand the process that triggers a habit (Event → Means (produces a feeling) → Learned Response → Positive

Reinforcement) you see that the best way to stop a habit from returning is to avoid the event/place/thing that triggers the thought that gets it going!

For example, if you're trying to stop the habit of drinking after work, you don't go to the bar after work anymore! However when it comes to eating and exercise habits, this would likely mean avoiding your kitchen, friends, family, and work—all common triggers for overeating and not exercising. So knowing this, you can clearly see why most fail at their resolutions and that more is needed to successfully change habits.

Step 2 - Take a New Action

When changing a program, it's important to understand what need the program was meeting so that you can find alternatives to meet that need rather than leave it unfulfilled. Without a replacement, your brain will be automatically drawn back to the old program to get the need met.

For example, if you decide you want to watch less TV and exercise more, you'll be more successful if you understand what needs watching TV was providing you. If your favorite shows were news programs, a need replacement could be to read the newspaper while riding the exercise bike at the gym to get that particular need met.

When it comes to eating and exercise habits, most unhealthy programs provide for the powerful emotional needs of comfort, reward, or control.

Comfort is the need of feeling good. Eating pleasure foods makes us feel good both physically and psychologically. We associate feelings of pleasure with certain foods—usually high in fat, carbs, or sugar. From our early years, we are given these types of foods at birthday parties and holidays.

Furthermore, carbs are our body's preferred source of energy, and fat provides the most calories for survival, so it makes sense we have a hard-wired comfort response to eating foods high in carbs and fat.

Some alternative ways to feel comfort are a hot shower, a nap, listening to music, reading, a favorite hobby, deep breathing, meditation, or writing.

Reward is the need to feel appreciated. Most of us don't get nearly the appreciation we crave so we often "feel like" rewarding ourselves and the easiest way to do this is with food and treats. Furthermore, many of us were conditioned as kids that good behavior and good work get a special treat like ice cream, cookies, or candy.

Some alternative ways to reward yourself are by writing in a journal what you accomplished each day and giving yourself praise for what you accomplished. Even easier is making a "to-do" list each day and checking the items off upon completion. By seeing on paper what you actually accomplished, you'll feel good about yourself: self-appreciation.

Perhaps the most powerful alternative is deciding to change your beliefs in regard to rewards and the ways in which you feel appreciated. Changing from the self-destructive belief that good work deserves good food to the new self-enhancing belief that good work deserves a good workout is something you can choose to start believing today. Just this one belief will completely change what you "feel like" doing.

It is also imperative that you understand that those who you'd like to appreciate you more also want you to appreciate them more. We all want appreciation, so the best way to feel appreciation is to give it, and watch it come back to you.

So, rather than appreciating yourself with food and treats, appreciate yourself by giving appreciation to others. This "give to get" approach seems counterintuitive, but it really works if you give it time to start coming back to you—often in larger quantities than you give.

For example, start to thank and appreciate those you work with. Just a sincere "thank you" when appropriate will start the appreciation flowing back to you.

Take control of your actions

Control is the need to have a choice. When you feel like everyone in your life is telling YOU what to do, it's hard to deny yourself the choice of doing what you "feel like" doing. This need can become a defiant attitude of:

"Why should I let others decide what I do, what I should weigh, or what I should eat?"

This can show up in your work life as well. If you resent your boss or client because you are unhappy with your job, you'll procrastinate on projects and put off important work as a means to gain control of the situation.

The lack of control in other areas of your life can lead to trying to control others at home. This always leads to friction because they want to have their own control, and are, at the same time, trying to control you. This need for control leads to arguments, fights, constant yelling and disrespect, all causing substantial stress, depression, anger, and resentment, drawing one strongly to find comfort in unhealthy habits like stress eating or substance abuse.

To avoid this force that destroys you and your loved ones, you must adopt a new belief that only you can, and should, control yourself. Trying to control others to feel good leads to massive amounts of pain and self-destruction.

By focusing on your own life, and letting others do more of what they want, you put your energy where it should be. When you are focused on your goals and what you want to accomplish, you don't have time or energy to get upset about how the towels in the bathroom were folded or become furious when your spouse forgets to put their plate in the dishwasher.

When you have control over exciting and compelling things in your life, you'll lose the need to constantly control others to feel satisfied with your life.

To find other things that will give you the feeling of control, make a list of things you would like to do to feel in control of your own life and begin to work on that list.

That list might include starting a part time business, learning sign language or a foreign language, or how to ride a motorcycle. It might include traveling to a foreign country or going back to school or running a half marathon.

Make sure you include easy things like "Read the paper alone every Sunday morning" or "Go to one movie a month" so you can start feeling more in control.

Awareness is the biggest challenge

To find an effective habit replacement, you need to identify what need your habit is providing for you. Because your programs run automatically, it can be difficult to identify the needs they are providing.

A person that bites their nails doesn't say to themselves, "Oh, I'm feeling nervous now. I think I will bite my nails to feel comfort because that always works for me," before they bite their nails.

A person with a hot temper program doesn't say to themselves, "Hey, that person just criticized me and that makes me feel bad, so I will criticize him back to feel better because that always works for me," before they yell at someone.

A person with a habit of eating while watching TV doesn't say to themselves, "Oh, my favorite TV program is on, I will get my bowl of chips because that always gives me pleasure," before they pour a bowl of chips.

When you ask a person about one of their habits by asking "why do you do that?" the most common response is: "ummm...I don't know, just because?" This shows just how invisible our programs are because of their subconscious operation. We don't consciously choose our habits, they just occur automatically.

The task of seeing your habit and finding a replacement requires self-awareness. This can present an initial challenge because self-awareness is something many folks have developed a habit of avoiding. If you don't really like what you see in the mirror, you easily develop a strong habit of avoiding looking in mirrors. But to change a program, you first have to become aware of it—see it for what it is, in order to make a good decision on what could replace it.

The more closely you can analyze your programs, the better you will be at finding effective replacements. Feeling comfortable and willing to look closely at why you do what you do is nothing less than essential for your success.

Almost everyone who wants to lose weight feels uncomfortable looking at themselves. This is where most fail. They'd rather try to force themselves to do something (like stop eating before bed) than to look in the mirror and find out why they feel so compelled to eat before bed, or to fix the cause for the behavior. This is where you use your willpower—to look in the mirror and see what's going on.

There are essentially two paths that you can follow:

> Stay unaware of why you have the habit and try, with all your willpower, to force yourself to change it. Or...

> Look in the mirror to find out why you have the problem so you can fix it by replacing it with a better alternative.

Most people choose the first path. Looking in the mirror is self-condemning and painful if you believe your brain's habits are your habits. However, once you separate your self-worth from your brain's habits, you become free to look in the mirror to find a solution by asking yourself these two questions:

> 1. What positive feeling or relief from discomfort (need) is this program giving me?

> 2. What could I start doing to provide the same positive feeling or relief from discomfort (same need)?

Not too many people fight changing to a newer car even though your car becomes a big habit in your life. Many identify themselves by the car they drive. But very few people have trouble trading in their old car for a new car. Why? Because the new car always provides better for their needs.

So when trying to find a new action to replace the need your old habit provided for you, if you can find something that provides for the need better or more effectively, you'll have a "New Car!"

A good idea might not instantly come to you, but don't give up. Use the internet to do a search like "Things to do instead of eating while watching TV" and see what ideas others have. Seeing others thoughts will stimulate your own ideas.

Also, I find my best ideas come to me when I am very relaxed, often in the shower, napping or driving. Keep asking yourself and a good idea will come.

Step it down

An excellent replacement strategy that makes total sense, but so few do, is the "step it down" strategy. This is simply dividing your replacement into progressive steps.

For example, let's say you want to stop your program of drinking Pepsi while working on the computer. You decide you want to replace it with drinking water.

Your brain might find jumping directly from sweet pop to water far too disappointing to create enough reinforcement to stick. In this case, you might be better off switching to diet soda for a month, then moving to flavored water, and then to water.

This strategy requires patience and a slow-but-sure approach to habit change. The reason most people don't use a step down strategy is because we all want results sooner, and we think our willpower works better than it really does.

After reading the first part of this book, you now know that you have only a finite amount of willpower with which to work.

So let me ask you this very important question:

Wouldn't you rather take your time, enjoy the process AND get results rather than overwhelm yourself, feel loads of discomfort, and most likely fail?

This is probably the best bit of advice I can give you for changing any of your habits. Only when you reinforce your new actions through experiencing positive reinforcement will they stick and become your new habits!

Trying to go too fast or change too much at one time always creates too much discomfort, causing the lack of reinforcement of the new actions.

I would rather change one habit every two months and have six habits changed at the end of the year than try to change 23 habits in a week, overwhelm myself and fail at all of them. This is what millions of people keep trying to do every January.

Trying to change too much too fast almost always fails, and then most folks blame their own willpower, which disempowers them and sets them up for more future habit change failure!

Only when you reinforce your new actions through experiencing positive reinforcement will they stick and become your new habits.

Replacement must provide pleasure

Julie loves eating snacks every evening while watching TV. She knows this is one of the reasons she can't lose weight, so she decides to replace watching TV in the evening with paying bills, doing taxes, and other paper work.

Julie thinks that by doing the paperwork, she'll get tons of satisfaction reinforcement because she always procrastinates with paperwork and it will feel good to get this stuff done.

For a week, she forces herself to do paperwork even though she finds herself thinking about watching TV and eating snacks. Eventually Julie slips-up and decides to watch her favorite show and open a bag of nachos.

Because she hasn't done this in a week, the pleasure she experiences is high, strongly reinforcing the pleasure associated with the old program in her brain. From this slip-up, she decides that this habit is just "who she is" and tells herself she'll find some other way to lose weight.

Julie's association: Evenings → watch TV and eat snacks → enjoyment and relief from her stress & disappointments

New association that didn't work: Evenings → do paperwork & bills → not fun, no enjoyment or stress relief.

When deciding on a new replacement, be sure to find replacements that bring pleasure and provide as closely as you can for the need being met by the old habit.

A better replacement for Julie might have been to join a gym and go exercise after dinner, or purchase an exercise bike to watch TV while biking in the evenings.

Pleasure is a Perception

It is very important that you understand and believe that what you experience comes from you and not the object you find either pleasurable or unpleasant.

A carrot is neither delicious nor repulsive. Only a person can create either perception of a carrot.

If you hate carrots, it may seem odd for me to tell you that you are choosing to perceive a carrot as distasteful, but that's exactly what you are doing. The carrot itself does not taste bad or good. Proof of this is other people just like you perceive carrots as tasting good.

The point is that you and anyone can CREATE pleasure within your own thinking for things you previously found displeasing.

Anything you currently don't "like" you can flood your head with thoughts of pleasure while experiencing it to reprogram your brain to like that thing.

You can program your brain to like ANY healthy food or activity because pleasure is a perception that you can change. This is an essential belief and skill for habit change.

Step 3 - Remove the Positive Reinforcement

A program thrives and becomes stronger each time you run it because of the positive reinforcement you receive each time. Without this positive reinforcement, the behavior would never have become a habit or stay a habit. Therefore, an effective strategy to eliminate an unwanted program is to remove the positive reinforcement the program provides. This can be done in two ways:

1. Give the benefit the habit provides a new painful meaning

2. Associate a painful consequence to the habit

For example, John loves going out to eat with his friends on Friday nights, and he always eats and drinks until he is full and satisfied. The positive reinforcement of this habit is the social aspect of being with friends and the feeling of satisfaction from eating and drinking until becoming very full.

A new painful meaning of the social aspect need might be that those people he's socializing with don't care about their health and are programming John to accept that overeating and living overweight is normal and OK.

If John wants to lose weight and live a healthier lifestyle, he will now see the social aspects of going out to eat with his friends as detrimental to his goals.

Furthermore, he can redefine the benefit of feeling satisfied when he is feeling full to feeling unsatisfied with himself, because having a full stomach is making him overweight and extinguishing his goals.

The second method involves bringing your attention to the painful consequences of running your program so that you move away from the old program. A classic example is when a person gets in an accident from driving after drinking, and thus, a new negative consequence of drinking now pushes them away from their habit of drinking and driving.

.Old association: Friday night → go out and drink beer → enjoyment with friends

New association: Go out and drink beer → nearly killed someone from being drunk!

New program that develops: Friday night → stay home and watch Sports on TV → avoid drinking, enjoy sports on TV

To create this in your life, you must use your conscious thinking to vividly picture the potential pain and discomfort that could come from continuing the program.

The longer you think about something, the more real it becomes. For example, you could associate any food you eat after 8:00 pm as turning directly into gross, wrinkly, cellulose fat on your legs!

The more often you think about this, the more you picture it. The more you picture it, the more your subconscious brain will believe it, and the more it will help you break your habit, because your brain now associates not only the pleasure of eating, but also the painful picture of having ugly legs!

Because of our natural human tendency to avoid what we don't want to believe, this strategy takes some effort. However, the effort is well worth it.

Eliminating the positive reinforcement of your habits is like taking their wheels off—they just can't move without them! Furthermore, finding and believing in powerful negative consequences can make change nearly instantaneous as opposed to taking weeks or months!

Often times we live life unaware of the consequences of our own behaviors, but when brought to light, they become powerful motivators.

Step 4 - Re-Program Your Subconscious

What compels you, what we call "habits," originates in the powerful subconscious function of your brain. You consciously resolve to start eating bananas for your afternoon snack, but when 3:00 rolls around, you feel powerfully compelled to forgo your resolution and buy a snickers bar from the vending machine.

Where does this compelling force that opposes our conscious wishes and makes us feel hopeless come from?

As you now know, it's not a thought you have, but a thought produced from a program within your subconscious brain. In this case, the program comes from the past experiences that a candy bar has always provided you pleasure this time of day.

That emotion of pleasure is imprinted into your nervous system and associated with the candy bar and the time of day.

This is the compelling force we are all trying to overcome to better our lives.

Easier than you think

Many people think the brain and human behavior is far too complex for the average person to comprehend. After all, studies have found the brain is more powerful than 100 super computers combined. It allows us to see, hear, move, talk, remember, and regulate our bodies, which is nothing less than a multi-functional miracle. But when it comes to guiding our behavior, your subconscious brain operates by a simple learn-and-do method.

Your brain operates on what is recorded in its memory as beliefs. What you "experience" you place a meaning on, which is then recorded as a belief. The brain operates in the future from this belief.

The more similar experiences you have, the more that certain belief is reinforced. An experience can be an event like losing your job, which might cause several beliefs like life isn't fair, I can't get out of this rut, etc.

Thankfully, you don't need to know every belief your brain is holding that is guiding your current behavior. What you do need to know is how to program the new belief you want your brain to operate by.

Your conscious thinking is the gatekeeper to what becomes programmed into your subconscious. Only what you consciously believe to be true will be programmed. Your subconscious mind has absolutely no ability to reason or think things out. It simply records the beliefs you consciously provide it and acts on them.

This can be illustrated by the power of suggestion. Suppose a timid looking passenger is in the seat next to you on the plane and you say to her something like this: You look pale. I'm sure you're getting sick. Here, take this bag so you have something for when you throw up.

The passenger turns pale, and your suggestion of airsickness associates itself with her own fears and apprehensions. She accepts the bag and shortly after takeoff, your negative suggestion, which was accepted by her, is realized.

However, that same suggestion could be made to the stewardess aboard the plane and produce a totally different outcome. The stewardess would probably laugh or smile at your suggestion of airsickness, because her own immunity from it is associated in her mind. For her, it calls up not fear and worry, but self-confidence.

The point is, whatever your conscious mind (you) agrees with, can be programmed into your subconscious. What you don't agree with cannot. Your conscious mind (your thinking) is the gatekeeper of what is programmed into your subconscious.

Whatever you believe will be programmed into your subconscious!

To get the subconscious to do what you want, you must either bypass your conscious mind, or get it to believe what you want.

Hypnotists do this sort of thing all the time. They bypass the conscious mind to directly program the subconscious mind to do things the conscious mind would normally reject. It can be awfully amusing to see people follow commands to jump up and dance and do other funny things under hypnosis when their conscious mind is not active and unable to disagree with the suggestion. It also shows you the power of your subconscious mind.

A similar effect occurs when we sit or lie peacefully and relax our bodies and minds into a meditative state—like what occurs before sleep. Your conscious mind is much less active, and therefore, more agreeable to your suggestions.

The term "autosuggestion" is used to describe this skill of making suggestions to yourself to program your subconscious for personal betterment. It can also be called affirmation or Self-Talk.

You are actually doing this all the time as you talk to yourself through your internal voice (thinking), giving meaning to all the events you experience during the day.

Autosuggestion is a very powerful tool to program your subconscious to do what you want it to do. It uses the same power that allows a hypnotist to get a person to dance with a broom; surely you can use its power to get yourself to eat a banana as your preferred afternoon snack.

Why willpower fails

So you make a resolution to eat a banana after work to replace the chips, cookies, or crackers you usually eat upon arriving home. What happens when you arrive home on that first day after you made your resolution?

Your subconscious will start pumping out internal thoughts (the voice you hear in your head) like dieting really sucks, or that you can't do it, or other negative thoughts that are keeping you from your goals.

These statements that "spring up" come from your current subconscious associations or habits. Without your conscious rebuttal, they will become suggestions reinforcing the program of eating junk food after work.

Trying to use willpower to force yourself to eat the banana while hearing the barrage of statements that produce feelings away from the banana and back toward the old habit proves to be impossible for most people—and for good reason—it is darn near impossible. This is why willpower nearly always fails.

Empower Your Willpower

Through the use of your own conscious Self-Talk rebuttal, you can override the power of your subconscious voice. You can either think your rebuttal or say your rebuttal out loud.

For example, while eating the banana, you say silently to yourself, "I love eating bananas because they make me healthy, and that feels good." At the same time your subconscious voice is saying: "This sucks, I'd rather have chips and dip!"

The two opposing thoughts essentially neutralize each other allowing you to choose.

Using a rebuttal affirmation while eating the banana prevents a negative feeling of deprivation from popping up and pulling you back to eating the chips and dip.

Remember, the law of reinforcement says that anything to be reinforced must cause pleasure and not pain. The absence of pain allows the feeling of pleasure to develop in the case of choosing a healthier food to eat.

Think of your subconscious mind like an elephant. Very powerful, but it will only do what it knows. Once you have re-programmed it to do what you want, that power will work for you!

To enhance your affirmation's power to change your programming, say your affirmation out loud. You might initially feel too self -conscious to think you can do this, but once you prove the power of audible Self-Talk, you'll understand exactly what I mean.

As an experiment, say silently to yourself with enthusiasm:

"I'm going to have a GREAT day!"

Now say the same affirmation out loud with the same enthusiasm.

Feel the difference?

The difference you "felt" is the enhanced emotion you'll feel with the added sense of hearing. Hearing is the most powerful sense we have for experiencing emotion. What people say to you through spoken word and music can instantaneously cause you to experience deep emotions.

Emotion is what moves you! Emotion is energy. The emotion associated with past experiences is what gives your habits control over your behavior. The more emotion, the more power to compel you.

Hearing is the most powerful sense we have for experiencing emotion.

To say that audible affirmations produce more emotion than silent affirmations is like saying a campfire produces more heat than a candle. Silent affirmations have their place and are helpful when you are around others and don't want to explain why you are talking out loud to yourself.

However, becoming comfortable with and learning to regularly use audible self-talk will become an essential tool enabling you to break any old limiting habits much faster and with much more success.

Autosuggestion, Affirmations, and Self-Talk

Autosuggestion is a word to describe making a suggestion to your subconscious. An affirmation is also an autosuggestion but is usually something positive you affirm about yourself or who you want to be.

For example, "I'm a problem solver" or "I love to exercise." Autosuggestions are often suggestions for wanted behavior like: "I always write in the mornings" or "I always go to the gym after work." Self-Talk encompasses both terms describing the skill of talking to yourself for a positive programming benefit. Although all terms are intermingled, I'll use the traditional term autosuggestion here.

How to use autosuggestion

Make your suggestions present tense. This means statements like "I am...," or "I never...," or "I know..." The purpose of your suggestion is to paint a picture in your brain of you already having the desired behavior.

Example: "I'm a successful entrepreneur" or "I always bring healthy foods to work" or "I never smoke." The exception to the rule of present tense is when facing a situation in which you want to guide your behavior or how you feel by using future tense language like "I will..." or "I'm going to...."

For example: "I'm going to enjoy this day with the in-laws" or "I'm going to choose an apple when I get home from work."

Make your suggestion simple. Just like a suggestion to someone to "always wear your seat belt" is going to be more successful than "always wear your seat belt when it is snowing or raining and drive under the speed limit with the radio off and the cruise control off and look for deer."

Focus your suggestion on one simple direction you want to impress upon your brain to follow. Make it simple and direct.

Make your suggestion believable. If your suggestion is not believable to you, it won't be programmed into your subconscious. To be "believable," all you need is to believe in its possibility.

For example, the suggestion "At dinner, I will eat from a small plate and not take seconds" is believable because you know you could do this. A suggestion like "I love eating salads for lunch" when you absolutely dislike salads won't work.

A better suggestion to start with would be: "I'm learning to like salads" or "I love to try all foods." Later, you can step-up to the "I love eating salads" suggestion.

Furthermore, it is important that you are in a relaxed or "feel good" state when you make your suggestions to make them believable. If you are upset or feeling down, your suggestion will likely be rejected because your negative attitude gives you a negative perspective. Remember, mood affects willpower.

Make your suggestion often. The more often you make a suggestion to your brain, the more it becomes programmed.

For example, if you're trying to establish the habit of strength training, you can verbalize a suggestion like "I love working my muscles" while showering and thinking about your day ahead, while driving to work and thinking about your impending workout, on your way to the gym, at the gym while working out, on your drive home from the gym, and at home when your workout comes to mind while you're eating dinner.

The more often you suggest a new belief to your brain, the faster and more strongly you'll program that new belief into your subconscious.

Save your most difficult habits for suggestions prior to sleep. Getting yourself into a highly relaxed sleepy state quiets your conscious brain and allows for greater acceptance of your most difficult suggestions.

For example if you've been overweight your entire adult life, the suggestion of "I am thin and healthy" might be rejected by your conscious brain, but in a pre-sleep state your consciousness is lowered and it will be more likely to reach your subconscious.

Proof of this is that suggestions like "I can fly" prior to sleep can cause a person to have dreams of flying. Your subconscious brain does not share the same limits your conscious self does. It knows no limits—only you limit yourself by your own conscious thinking!

This is what is really exciting about your subconscious brain. Yes, it takes some work, and you'll have to get past the initial strange feeling of talking to yourself. However, getting your subconscious brain that knows no limits to start working for you is worth every bit of effort—the payoff potential is off the charts.

Your Success Plan

Successfully reprogramming your subconscious to stop doing what you don't want and start doing what you want takes two actions:

> 1. Become aware of and talk back to your brain's negative thoughts

> 2. Create a plan of self-talk suggestions to reprogram what you want

The most important part of your success is becoming aware of the self-defeating, negative internal voices and talking back to them when they pop-up. A word I really like for the constant thoughts in your head is "mind chatter."

Because these thoughts are just a constant flow of reactions and thoughts based on fear, insecurity, past mistakes, painful memories, and a whole bunch of other stuff recorded in your subconscious, it isn't worth listening to. It's nothing more than a bunch of "chatter" that gets in your way of making good decisions for your life.

Remember your subconscious brain's number one job is to keep you out of danger, and it does that through mind chatter! Mind chatter is the voice that reminds you of what could go wrong, why you could fail, your faults, your inabilities, your past failures, etc.

Your brain wants to keep you stuck in the past because that's all it knows.

Becoming aware of how you are currently letting your mind chatter affect you and then talking back to it, you begin to neutralize the power it has had over you and what you do.

Why can't I just ignore my mind chatter?

Just becoming aware of or "seeing" your mind chatter, you have won half the battle!

You'll be able to see how foolish, limiting, and nonsensical it is, and you'll be compelled to stop following it! If you hear "you are not smart enough to do that" and you are aware of that voice as just being your own mind chatter, you are free to decide consciously what you want to do.

Most people live their lives hearing their mind chatter and thinking it's their thinking. They act on it because they see it as truth. A person who is not aware of their mind chatter and hears "you are not smart enough to do that" will believe it and feel it emotionally, and that will control what they do.

However, just becoming aware of your mind chatter doesn't change it. It's simply the first step to stop its powerful influence over how you feel, and what you do. But our goal is to get rid of the mind chatter that keeps influencing you.

Your mind chatter is your subconscious programming being shown to you. It presents a "golden opportunity" to see the problem and correct it! Why would we let that pass us by? When you hear "you're not smart enough to do that," you're hearing your subconscious programming, and the book is literally open to that page of your brain, giving you the opportunity to write on that page what you'd rather have pop up next time!

Immediately, if you say with your own strong Self-Talk, "I am smart enough to do a lot of things and what I don't know I learn," you now record a new belief and feeling on that same page.

Will this change your programming instantly? No. But next time, that new belief and feeling you just wrote on the same page will get pulled up along with the old negative belief, and you won't feel as compelled to follow the old belief! Each time you use strong, positive Self-Talk immediately after you hear and feel your mind chatter, you keep weakening the old negative belief and its effect on you.

Your mind chatter is your subconscious programming being shown to you. It presents a "golden opportunity" to see the problem and then correct it!

Listen for and become sensitive to negative beliefs about yourself and your abilities. When you hear your brain say things like "I always screw up" or "I just can't control myself" or "I suck at this", these are negative beliefs about yourself.

When you hear your brain say things like "I hate green beans" or "Exercise sucks!" or "I'm a mess!", these are negative beliefs about things. Below are examples of what you could say to talk back to your mind chatter:

What your BRAIN said:	What YOU should say:
"I ALWAYS screw up"	"I am learning a lot.... that feels so good!"
"I just CAN'T control myself"	"I CAN control myself... that feels so good!"
"I'll always be a big girl"	"I can be whatever I want to be... it feels so good to know that!"
"I HATE Beets"	"I am learning to Love healthy foods.. I am so proud of that!"
"Getting up early sucks!"	"Getting up early makes me successful... I love that feeling!"
"I NEED a slice of pie!"	"I control food... I am accomplishing my goals and that feels so awesome!"
"Wow, that looks delicious"	"I Love how I LOOK more than what food looks like... that makes me feel so good!"

Yes, it is that simple and easy to de-program your old negative self-destructive beliefs that continually pop up, holding you back from what you really want. It takes time and patience, but if you develop the habit of using forceful, positive Self-Talk rebuttals to your negative mind chatter, you will soon see a shift in your mind chatter, how you feel, and what you do.

Make your Self-Talk rebuttals feel good!

Notice my suggested statements in the preceding chart all end with statements of positive feelings like "it feels so good." Remember, the power of a word is the feeling it causes. A statement creating a "feel good" feeling powerfully draws your brain toward it, and thus magnifies its power to make an impression on your subconscious programming.

Adding enthusiasm in your voice and body movements, like making a fist or raising an arm in the air, add to the emotional impact of your Self-Talk affirmation. Prove this to yourself by reading one of the statements in the above chart silently to yourself. Then read the next statement out loud in a monotone voice. Then read the next statement out loud with enthusiasm. Then read the next statement out loud, with enthusiasm and with body movement like making a fist or pumping an arm in the air.

The power of a word is the feeling it causes.

Self Talk Affirmation	Power
Say silently in your head	Good
Say out loud	Better
Say out loud with enthusiasm	Very Good
Say out loud with enthusiasm with body movement	Best

Which one FEELS most powerful? Did the last one give you goose bumps, or did you feel a tingle of energy flow through your body? When you create a strong emotion, you will feel it in your body! Emotion is the energy that imprints your subconscious. Greater energy = greater imprint. Greater imprint means greater change!

> **Key Point #1:** You can't put out a fire by dismissing and refusing it, you have to put water on it. Similarly, you can't put out your mind chatter without action. Your own Self Talk is the "water" that puts out the fire of your mind chatter!

> **Key Point #2:** The sooner you put water on the fire, the easier it is to put it out. If you wait too long, the fire will grow so large, your Self-Talk won't work!

It is very important that you become aware of your mind chatter, and talk back to it before it grows in your head. This is the "core" skill that makes successful habit change possible. Try, practice, and then master it, and you will have success!

Your personality habit

I have found a definite correlation between personality type and success at implementing the strategies for successful habit change. To understand what I am talking about, answer this question:

If someone at work blames you for something you didn't do, do you:

> a) Confront the person and prove that you didn't do what you were blamed for

> b) Complain to others privately or to yourself about unfair people at work or not say anything so as not to upset the boat, fearing you might lose your job

Because successful habit change involves identifying and talking back to your subconscious programing, type-A people are more successful in doing what needs to be done to change habits.

Furthermore, type-B people have higher levels of fear. They fear many things—what people would think, what could happen, what happened before, what if, what if?

These folks listen to, believe, and follow their mind chatter more than do type-A people. Because type-B people take their mind chatter more literally, it grows in frequency and power over their lives from the reinforcement they give it.

Type-B folks must understand that their personality is just a habit developed over the years to escape discomfort and pain, and they can choose to be type-A just by starting to identify and talk back to their mind chatter.

Think of having a person following you around 24/7 always telling you negative, self-limiting things that bring you down. That person's name is "mind chatter!"

How would you handle this?

A Type-B person would avoid conflict and just accept what the person says and thus stay stuck in those habits. A Type-A person would stand up against what that person was saying, rejecting it with strength and conviction.

If you have a hard time standing up to others with strength and conviction, realize that you'll need to use your willpower to start standing up to your mind chatter. The secondary benefit of doing this is you'll start standing up for yourself in other areas of your life, too, giving your self-confidence and self-esteem a mega-boost.

Identifying your current personality type is not meant to make you feel bad or provide another perceived character flaw with which to judge yourself negatively.

If you are a type-B personality, the last thing you need is something else to criticize yourself with. Most of us were taught that humility and meekness are good virtues. As children, the first thing many of our parents instilled in us through their parental control is the belief that standing up for what we want is unacceptable.

Keep in mind that most people are "type-B" personalities. So type-B isn't "bad," it's just not what you need to stand up and defeat the programming that is keeping you from the life you really want.

Strength training makes you a strong person. That does not mean nasty and arrogant, it means of strong character and personality—able to take on and push through challenges.

Strength training makes you feel strong, and when you feel strong, you can stand up to those internal voices that say you're a loser, you'll fail, or that you'll never change.

Step 5 - Visualize Your Success

Visualization is the act of picturing something in your mind. It utilizes the incredible power of your imagination. Your brain is visualizing all the time.

When you think about someone, you visualize them. When you think about something fun you did last weekend, you are visualizing it. When you think about going to the store to get groceries, you visualize the store you are thinking about going to. The process of thinking is really visualization.

Your brain thinks in pictures. Now that you know that your brain's main job is to protect you from harm and danger, what pictures do you think are produced most often? Your mind chatter is mostly in the "what could go wrong" category, so your brain is busy creating pictures of what could go wrong much more often than it is creating pictures of what could go right.

Self-Talk creates visualization. When you say "I like dogs," you will automatically visualize a dog. When you say "I like to try new foods" as a rebuttal to your negative mind chatter of "I hate tuna," you may picture yourself trying the tuna.

The difference between Self-Talk and visualization is that visualization takes the picture your Self-Talk creates and makes it more of a vivid and "real" experience, thus increasing the imprint on your subconscious.

Advertisers know the power of what you visualize all too well! Notice how most food commercials are close-up pictures of the food. When you see the food, it becomes a real experience, as if it's sitting in front of you making your subconscious want it.

The power and benefit of visualization is that it creates an "experience." You can take a real hammer and pound a real nail into a board. Or you can imagine yourself taking a hammer and pounding a nail into a board.

Both register as "experiences" in your subconscious brain. Your subconscious cannot distinguish between a "real" experience and a visualized one.

This is why successful athletes visualize themselves making the goal. Roger Bannister is a great example of the power of this technique. When he was coming up as an athlete, it was considered impossible for a human being to run a four minute mile. It had never been done. There was no basis for the belief in reality.

But Roger set a goal to do just that. He visualized and constantly rehearsed the event over and over in his head until his mind and his body reflexively responded to his vision…and he broke the four-minute barrier. (Within a year of his success, 37 other runners accomplished the same feat.)

Using visualization works really well with things you have been unsuccessful at—like trying to change a habit.

For example, let's say you've tried choosing carrots while watching the game on TV, but you always find a bowl of chips sitting on your lap. Visualization helps you record successful "experiences" in doing what you consciously want, which then reprograms your brain toward doing what you want.

After a week of visualizing eating carrots and other healthy snacks, and enjoying them while watching the game, when you go to actually do this, your subconscious thinks: "Heck, I've done this before, this is normal" and you won't feel the automatic rejection of the carrots.

Visualization helps you become successful in doing what you consciously want by planting successful experiences into your subconscious

Visualization can also be used to create powerful emotional associations to help a person move away from old programming and toward a new behavior. For example, if you want to stop eating before bed, you can visualize every bite of food turning into fat on your face and using visualization to create a compelling movie in your head of people seeing your fat face, making fun of you, your kids being ashamed of you, etc.

Because it's your imagination, you can get as creative as you want to, effectively associating pain to the old habit and pleasure to the new behavior you are trying to establish.

To create a more powerful pull toward the new behavior, you could visualize your kids being proud of you, receiving an award with all your peers applauding you, or getting an unexpected promotion at work. Think of and use things that matter to you so they make you feel really awesome!

Example: Kathy wanted to establish a love for lifting weights in the gym. She had always just used the treadmill and was never serious about the weights, until she learned her lack of strength training was a big reason she wasn't seeing the results she wanted.

Kathy decided that while she was lifting weights, she would envision herself in a new, strong body and the positive reactions of all of her colleagues at work to her new, strong self.

She envisioned contributing more during meetings and breaking past her shyness and how awesome that made her feel. At night before bed, she would visualize her workout, seeing every detail of her fit healthy body lifting weights in the gym. She envisioned herself giving other women advice and help—it felt so good to her to finally feel noticed and to feel valuable.

Using visualization helped Kathy establish a strong love for strength training in just a few months. In less than six months, her vision actually came true! She found herself helping two women she worked with to start strength training, and she was asked by her boss to start and manage a new wellness program. Kathy's first wellness class topic was entitled: "Why women should love lifting weights."

Visualization helps you in two important ways:

1 Helps you to develop confidence in doing something you want to be successful at, and

2. Helps you program emotional associations to what it is you want to change

How to use visualization effectively

To make visualization a powerful tool in your life, follow these five guidelines:

1. Make your visualizations as real as possible.

Real experiences include everything you saw, heard, smelled, felt, and even tasted. By imagining more details, you create an experience that seems real to your brain.

For example, if you want to visualize yourself on a beach, you would imagine not only what you see on the beach, but the sounds of the waves, the seagulls, people laughing, kids playing in the water, a distant stereo playing, etc.

You would also feel the chair under your body, the sand going through your toes, the sun warming your skin, the breeze going over your body.

You would also smell the sea air, the grill smoke from a restaurant, and perhaps the faint smell of sunscreen as someone close by lathered up.

You could also taste the cool, refreshing drink you have by your chair. The more details you imagine, the more real it will feel to you, and the greater will be the imprint on your subconscious.

2. Visualize the wanted outcome and the wanted new behaviors.

You want to visualize two things. The outcome and what you need to do to get the outcome.

For weight loss, you would visualize yourself thin and healthy along with all the positive feedback and how you would feel. Visualizing the wanted outcome convinces your subconscious mind that what you want is possible, thus making your efforts seem worthwhile and normal.

You would also visualize what you need to do to get to that goal, which would be the specific things you must do like choosing an apple over chips. Choosing to go to bed hungry rather than full.

Visualizing the actions to get your desired result (eating green beans instead of chips) help these actions feel more "normal" and less painful to your brain, making their successful implementation easier and faster.

3. Set up a time to practice important visualizations.

If you want to harness this power in your life, you'll need to set up a routine time to visualize. A great time to visualize is before falling asleep. When you shut off all other sensory input, your visualization takes center stage with your subconscious mind.

So instead of thinking about things that worry or upset you, visualize yourself successfully choosing the apple over the bag of chips—and how good you feel doing it.

Visualize the details of yourself successfully enjoying a book in the evening, rather than a bowl of ice cream—and how proud and smart you feel.

Visualize the details of walking on a tropical beach looking and feeling fantastic in a swimsuit, or the details of walking into work feeling healthy, strong and successful.

4. Use visualization to control your emotions.

When you feel anxious, stressed, or worried, use positive visualization to combat the feelings that hurt you and your potential to make positive life changes. These feelings are just your brain creating negative pictures of what might, could, should, or may happen.

It is all imaginary!

So do away with this imaginary chatter that is hurting you with your own imaginary thoughts! Visualize things working out. Visualize people doing the opposite of what you're worrying about. Visualize something totally funny or crazy! This will instantly change how you feel, because you can't visualize two things at the same time.

For example, let's say you are anxious and stressed because you forgot to pay the phone bill, and you imagine your husband being furious about the $20 late fee. You could escape this negative feeling by visualizing his head three times as big as normal and his voice in a funny high tone saying, "Hey, don't worry about that $20, mistakes happen." Then see him turn and skip away.

Repeat this visualization a couple times and you'll be laughing out loud and no longer allowing your brain to hurt you. You can use this trick anytime you feel any kind of stress or pain.

Somebody honks their horn at you, and you feel bad because you weren't paying attention. Instead of feeling guilty that you almost caused an accident, visualize the other person's car full of circus clowns or something else equally ridiculous.

Whatever scenario would make you laugh and feel better, create it in your thinking through visualization. Get into this habit, and you'll have an uncommon control of your emotions like no one else.

5. Keep your visualizations positive.

Don't visualize negative things - like your boss getting fired or other people experiencing pain. You want your subconscious to operate by peace and love for others, because that's how it will operate toward you.

If you have hatred toward others, your subconscious will also have hatred toward you. If you have hateful thoughts, know that you must reject them as unwanted programming, because that same destructive energy in your subconscious programming is doing you more harm than anyone else possibly could.

Step 6 - Putting It All Together

The best way to approach any change is to make it as easy as possible. Since easy is a perception, the thought of changing a habit as a trial takes away the pain of perceived permanence.

You are only committing to try it for a certain period of time to see what happens. When you think of forgoing your old program of eating cereal before bed for a seven-day trial period, to see how it goes, it feels easier to you and your brain than vowing to forgo this habit permanently.

Of course this is what you want, but by allowing the possibility of restarting the habit, you're allowing time to pass causing your habit's appeal to weaken from a lack of reinforcement.

Think of your subconscious brain as a seven-year old kid. It's easier to ask him to just start something than complete something.

At the end of the first trial period, you can go for a second trial period. Once you have gone about 14-30 days with just a few slip-ups, you should feel much more in control of the old program.

Now you're ready to run a 14-30 day "Commitment" period in which you try to limit slip-ups to none or just a few. You follow this with a 14-30 day "New me" time period. By the end of your "New Me" time period, your old habit should be fully behind you and you should "feel like" doing the replacement action.

You then sign your sheet: "The new me for life, this is who I am," and move to your next program. The path for successful program change looks like this:

Path for Successful Program Change	
Step #1:	7-14 Day "Trial" (with allowed slip-ups)
Step #2:	7-14 Day "Trial" (with fewer allowed slip-ups)
Step #3:	14-30 Day "Commitment" (goal is no slip-ups)
Step #4:	14-30 Day "New me" (no slip-ups)
The New Normal	

How long does it take to change a program?

There are many opinions on how long it takes to change a habit ranging from instantly to two years. Answering this question depends on a number of factors including:

> The emotional power of the program
>
> The amount of pain associated with the program
>
> The use of an effective replacement
>
> The use of autosuggestion
>
> The use of visualization

I think an equally important question to ask is: What are my chances of successfully changing a habit? If we know, for instance, that we'll be successful in 60 days, we'll stick with the new program for 60 days. But if we're not sure, it's easy to slip back into our old routine. Nobody wants to put two months of effort into something for nothing! We've all experienced this in the past.

Although it's impossible to tell you exactly how long it should take for a particular habit to change, I do know for certain that the more tools you use, the more likely you will be successful, and the faster you'll notice change.

The following chart illustrates my point:

Methods used	Chance of Success/Days to change*	
Stop running the program only	10%	120 days
Stop running the program with a replacement	20%	90 days
Associate pain to the old program	50%	30 days
Use auto suggestion	60%	25 days
Use visualization	70%	20 days

*estimates reflect the author's opinion and are used to illustrate the effectiveness of using additional methods

As you can see, just using willpower to change a habit doesn't have a very good probability of success. Yet millions of people keep trying every

January. Note that associating pain to the old program helps you the most. This illustrates your brain's powerful pain-avoidance propensity.

Spending time finding, creating, and then magnifying painful associations to your old program will pay the largest dividends toward your success. You can then use autosuggestions and visualization to program these painful associations, as well as the pleasure of the new behavior you want, to speed up the process of changing the habit as well as increasing the chance that it will stick.

Of course a person's level of effort determines their results—always has, always will. However, I want you to clearly see that by utilizing these simple additional skills, your likelihood of success goes from "not likely" to "very likely."

Most of all, trying to change a habit before you learn how to use pain avoidance, autosuggestion, and visualization is useless and counterproductive. If you are trying to change a habit, don't even try unless you use these additional tools, because you'll likely fail, and failure reinforces the habit, making it stronger.

Emotion—the glue of habits

Think of emotion as the "glue" that "sticks" a habit to you. The more glue, the harder it is to unstick yourself. The emotion associated with the habit will determine how long it will take for it to change.

Changing the route you drive to work could be changed in just a few days after you move to a new home, because your driving route probably doesn't have much emotion attached to it.

Something that brings you pleasure, like eating snacks before bed, could take many weeks to change because your brain has made strong emotional associations of pleasure with this habit. Using all methods, especially the association of pain to the old habit, must be utilized to successfully change a habit with a strong emotional association.

Slip-ups are expected as you battle mind chatter from the old habit, and teach yourself the new replacement. Slip-ups are helpful because they teach you what triggers your old program. Slip-ups also help you learn the details of your old habit and just how strong the habit is, allowing you to develop your patience and modify your efforts.

If you are moving toward fewer slip-ups, that is success! Patience is the key! Take the belief that slip-ups are the doors you must go through to reach your destination. Getting frustrated with yourself will absolutely destroy your success.

To help you learn from the slip-up, make one of your own rules to write down what you learned from it, or start the trial period over. Most of all, become curious about your own behavior and what affects what you do, rather than becoming mad at yourself and missing this golden opportunity.

The power of the written word

Writing things down solidifies your whirling thoughts onto a piece of paper. This makes what you write more clear and memorable. Imagine if our founding fathers had just talked about the Declaration of Independence and never written anything down. Imagine if you just took out a verbal mortgage. Imagine if the bank employee just kept track of your balance in her head.

When you start to think about it, anything important must be written down, or it isn't very important!

By writing your habit/program change down, you state clearly what it is you plan to do. It is no longer an idea; it's now a plan of action. This makes a vast difference! A plan of action gives you a significant boost in motivation, and the clarity of writing it down removes any uncertainty in what you aim to accomplish.

The Declaration of Independence was signed by our founding fathers. Why did they sign it? By signing, they made a commitment. They committed themselves to the written words on that piece of paper even when they knew their lives would be in jeopardy from that point forward.

Without their signatures, it would only be words on a piece of paper. Their signatures made it a commitment, which gave the document its tremendous value and power. Your signature does the same!

Think of each habit you change as your own "Declaration of Independence." You may think it's unnecessary to write down your resolution, but it can help you on your way. Taking the time to write down what you want to do and how you plan to accomplish it takes some time and effort.

But not doing so will hinder your efforts. Ideas and thoughts come and go. A thought you had today will likely be gone tomorrow. Write it down and it will still be here tomorrow, next week, and next month. Writing it down makes the process concrete.

How many habits can I work on at one time?

The reason why nearly all diets and weight loss programs fail is because the person tries to change several long-lived habits all at the same time! This always causes an eventual overload and subsequent failure. The number of habits you can successfully take on depends on how much stress you experience in your life and your level of self-confidence.

A busy mom with three kids and a career she finds stressful would have a difficult time tackling more than one large habit at a time. Those with high levels of self-confidence and less stress might be able to successfully tackle two or three at the same time.

Self-confidence is the belief in one's own abilities. If you believe you will succeed, you'll have more energy to take on changing more habits.

However, one thing is true. The more habits you try to change simultaneously, the lower the probability for success. Considering how difficult changing just one habit is, you will be best off in the long run if you consider operating by the less is more philosophy.

Use comfort and success as your guide. If you are working on three habits and finding you're slipping up too much, drop down to two habits and put the third back on the "to-do" list for later.

It's also very important that you start with easier habits and save your most difficult habits for after you have developed your habit changing skills and self-confidence.

Remember it's 100% better to succeed at changing just one habit than to fail at changing many!

Preventing backsliding

A "back slide" occurs after you have been operating with the new program for a period of time, making you believe you were successful. Thus, a back slide can be very demoralizing. You can easily develop the belief that the old habit is just "who you are" because it came back after it should have been gone. Often, just accepting the old habit back into one's life becomes the easiest way to find peace of mind after a back slide.

To prevent this from happening to you, you must understand WHY a back slide occurs. Backsliding can only occur when inadequate pain was associated with the old habit. Without the association of pain, there is still an association of pleasure which may be there months or even years after the change!

Without an adequate association of pain to the old habit, your new program becomes only a current "preference" over the old habit. With the association of pain, the new program becomes the "only way."

For example, say you successfully changed your habit of eating pizza to eating your own homemade vegetable turkey chili. You haven't had an urge to eat or buy a pizza in over six months, but one day a friend comes over with three delicious-looking pizzas for the playoff game.

You decide to have a slice, and one slice turns into three, and you end up eating about 1,200 calories of pure carbs and fat! Your brain hooks back up with the old association of pleasure, and you find yourself hearing your mind chatter justifying bringing pizza back into your diet!

Backsliding can only occur when inadequate pain was associated with the old habit.

Had you associated painful thoughts with eating pizza like "pizza is loaded with fat and isn't healthy. I can either have pizza or choose to live healthy. I can't have both." These harsh thoughts would have popped up, helping to keep you from eating the pizza, or, at the very least, stopping at one slice.

You might have experienced this in your own life. Have you ever gone from loving a food to complete avoidance of it just from one painful event? It doesn't even have to be the food's fault.

A person can catch the stomach flu and experience intense stomach pain, and if the last thing she ate was a taco, a strong association between immense pain and tacos could be established. When a strong emotion of pain is associated with anything, your subconscious mind chatter won't let you go back to it.

Expect slip-ups

When it comes to long ingrained habits, there will always be slip-ups - particularly if the habit is associated with something that you must do to survive – like eating. You can't expect perfection when it comes to food and eating. In fact, I tell people you need a weekly slip-up meal, because it gives your body a needed contrast and boosts your metabolism by pulling it out of "starvation mode," which always occurs if you're losing weight.

If you have a slip-up, tomorrow is a new day, and any overeating you did will be gone in 24 hours. Thinking that one slip-up causes you to gain five pounds and destroys your weight loss for the week is simply not true.

Even if you have an all-out binge one night, you just get back to your healthy routine, and you'll easily be back to last week's weight, or even drop a pound because of the natural metabolism boosting effect that occurs from a binge.

It's only when you are too hard on yourself and have the unrealistic thought that perfection is necessary for success, that a slip-up will turn in to a back slide. And it's only from unnecessary frustration and a lack of choosing self-confidence that a slip-up will turn into several days of slip-ups, skipping exercise, and self-condemning feelings.

This is easily avoided by taking the proper, healthy and balanced perspective—that slip-ups will happen—just let them go and get back to feeling good and back to your healthy routine.

Your attitude determines your success

When you ask someone, "How's it going?" the usual response is either an unenthusiastic generic response of "good" or "hanging in there." I think the response "hanging in there" is an excellent way to describe the overall general attitude that is so common today.

Most people feel their lives are pretty much just a day-to-day existence. They don't feel they have the power to create significant change. It's really no wonder - studies have been done that have found that the average person has been told "no," or that they can't do something over 140,000 times before they turn 18!

From the time we are able to understand the word "no," our parents began programming us with what we can't do, what we shouldn't do, what we are not able to do, what we should settle with, and that we should not expect too much. But we parents have no other choice. We have to keep our kids from riding their bikes down the highway or drinking window cleaner just to try it.

A child who thinks she can do anything is an extreme risk to herself and others. As good parents just trying to raise good kids, we program in our kids a deep belief that the world is a place full of danger and disappointment. We teach them that they must be careful, keep the status quo, and avoid risk.

However, this is the exact opposite attitude you need to change a habit. Habits thrive when you feel lousy and weaken when you feel great. You know this. Remember the last time you had a great day, felt on top of the world, so you decided to clean your closet, eat an apple, or go for a walk? Remember the last day you couldn't wait to get home from work, take off your shoes and just "veg" in front of the TV with a bag of chips to get a little "stress relief?"

It doesn't take a PhD in human behavior to see that if your "feel great" days are rare compared to your "hanging in there" days, you're going to run into difficulty trying to change any habit.

One of the most important things you must do to be able to change your habits is to learn how to make yourself feel good by adopting the habit of having a positive attitude.

Getting a positive attitude is simple. All you need to do is choose to focus on the sunny side of life, all your blessings and the small things in life that give you happiness every day.

Choosing a positive attitude also requires consciously letting go of the habit of over-focusing on your imperfections, the few things that do go wrong, and comparisons with others.

Most people think feeling good or bad is a result of what happens to them, but it's really your habits of thinking about life (mostly given to you from parenting and our "hanging in there" culture) that causes that attitude.

Each day, you can wake up and simply choose a new positive, happy, grateful, "I can" attitude—and renounce any negative, pessimistic, complaining "I can't" attitudes. This can be done in less than a minute using this audible Self-Talk on your way to work:

"Today is going to be a great day! Because I choose to focus on the good things all around me and the many blessings in my life now and coming to me! Today is going to be a great day because... (list several reasons that make you happy)."

Yes, it is as simple as that! It focuses your thinking in the right place at the beginning of your day, which then builds on itself throughout the day. It allows you to have a positive attitude, which is simply the absence of a negative attitude, and is a must to succeed in every aspect of your life! Teach this to your children. They'll love it.

"I don't have time"

One of the biggest roadblocks for habit change success is the belief "I don't have time." I'd like to go to the gym, but I don't have time. I'd like to start a business, but I don't have time. I'd like to exercise more, but I don't have time. I should look for a better job, but I don't have time.

I should do more with my kids, but I don't have time. I should shop for better foods, but I don't have time. I should learn healthier recipes, but I don't have time.

A book could be filled with "I don't have time" excuses.

One of mind chatter's most powerful weapons against you making any positive change is the thought of "I don't have time." But it's really not a matter of time, it's a matter of not wanting to give up the habit of your current routine. Your current routine is a comfortable habit.

What breaks a person out of their routine?

Something either highly pleasurable or highly painful.

You will break your routine to go to the dentist if you have a toothache. You will break your routine to go to someone's house for Christmas dinner. Unless there is something compelling you, your brain loves to stick to the comfort of a routine.

To break past the "I don't have time" mind chatter, first see it just as it is—mind chatter. It's not reality, but just your brain's response to the potential of losing its comfortable routine and the fear of doing something different and thus unknown.

I don't have time is also the perfect excuse to get out of doing something you don't want to do. If someone asks you to give a speech at your child's school, you can say "Sorry, I wish I could but I just don't have the time," and what can they say?

It's such a perfect excuse it even convinces you! This perfect excuse is used repeatedly when it comes to exercise— especially in regard to joining a gym. In the case of joining a gym, it's really not time, but the avoidance of feeling inferior, judged, or failing that makes this excuse so frequently used.

Don't let this destructive mind chatter live long in your focus. Respond to it with your own strong Self-Talk about how important what you want to do is and how it would be MORE painful NOT to do what you want to do!

Feel the emotion. Emotion is the energy that eradicates negative mind chatter.

> Mind chatter: *I don't have time to go to the gym, I have to go home and...*
>
> Your possible response: *I go to the gym at 5:00 because I can't be a successful dad and also be an overweight dad. My workouts make me feel like a man and a good father.*

> Mind chatter: *I don't have time to cook a bunch of food, I have to wash clothes, do this, do that...*
>
> Your possible response: *I always make food for the week on Sunday afternoons because it is so important to live the way I want! Without having good food available during the week, it's too easy to eat junk.*

The habit that stands in your way of changing habits

In this book, I have introduced and outlined the top skills that, when used together, empower you to do what so few can do—tap into your willpower and successfully change your habits.

At this point, you've probably thought to yourself "this makes sense" or "I can see how that could work" or "I can see how that could help me." You may even feel excited about trying Self-Talk and Visualization, and feel a new sense of liberation knowing that your brain's mind chatter is not really your thoughts.

However, the sad truth is that most people who read this book will eventually allow their mind chatter to overcome their initial enthusiasm, causing this to be another "good idea" that is never implemented into their lives.

Why do most good ideas, even easy ones that make a lot of sense, never get implemented? Even when they seem so obviously beneficial?

This universal human behavior is well illustrated in taking a pill. What could be easier than taking a pill with the huge benefit of curing a disease or ailment?

Yet studies show, and we all know by experience, that just getting yourself to perform a new task as easy as taking a little pill can be challenging! This new behavior of taking a pill reaches near impossibility when we are instructed to take the pill more than once a day.

Are we human beings just irresponsible? If irresponsibility is not realizing the colossal power of our habits and subconscious programming that powers them to keep us doing the same thing, than yes, most people are irresponsible.

To implement the strategies in this book, you have to break your old habit of not using these strategies. You have to break your habit of never using audible Self-Talk for a purpose. You have to break your habit of never intentionally visualizing. You'll have to break your habit of not spending time thinking about and magnifying what negative, painful consequences your current habits are causing you now and into the future.

Here is the type of mind chatter your brain will start pouring out as you contemplate implementing the skills in this book:

> *"I can't talk to myself, that's too weird."*

> *"I don't have time to visualize stuff."*

> *"I don't need to write my habit changes down…I'll just do it in my head."*

> *"These are good ideas, but I can't do all this stuff."*

> *"When I go to bed, I just want to sleep. Visualization is too hard."*

Now that you uniquely know what so few people know—that your mind chatter is not your thoughts, but only the natural activity of your brain's programming, you can choose to renounce it with your own Self-Talk and keep moving forward in your best interest.

Renounce your mind chatter with your own confident and strong Self-Talk like:

> *"Of course this stuff seems difficult; if it was easy everyone would be doing it!"*

> *"Visualization sounds very powerful; I can't wait to use it in my life!"*

> *"Understanding that my mind chatter is not really my thoughts, I feel like I know a secret others don't know that frees my life…this is such cool stuff!"*

> *"This is really interesting; I want to learn more about how my subconscious brain works."*

"I am going to implement these strategies slowly and gradually without stressing myself out."

"Thank you, brain, for trying to protect me, but I'm going to do this anyway."

The gift of choice

You have been given the gift of choice. Most people live their lives as their internal programming and the genetic code guides them. You and I, however, can make choices. Where we live, what we do, who we make friends with, who we live with, what we eat, when we go to bed, and the list goes on and on.

Our lives are a series of choices. Your current life is the result of your past choices. Most of your choices are the same day after day because your brain likes routine—it's the way it was designed—to learn something and then repeat it automatically.

Once you learned how to drive, tie your shoes, brush your teeth, or eat a certain way, you just keep repeating it over and over, day after day. Habits make life easier because you no longer have to "think" about doing something, it just happens.

However, our habits can become such forces that they cause us to forget about and stop believing in the gift of choice we all possess! By the time we become adults, most of us feel we have very little choice. We begin to believe that everything around us is choosing for us.

How can I go back to school? I have kids. How can I look for a better job? I have to pay the bills. How can I go to the gym? I don't have time. How can I like broccoli? I've always hated broccoli. How can I stop eating fast food for lunch every day? All my friends go there!

If you look closely, all these thoughts at the core have fear as the compelling emotion. Fear produces mind chatter and mind chatter extinguishes the gift that creates the life you really want: Choice. Once you believe this and start living your life by Your Choice, you will unlock the power that has always been within you to live a healthy life of success and happiness, in whatever way you choose to define it.

Putting It All Together

Life has moments that feel as if the sun has blackened to tar and the entire world turned to ice. It feels as if Hades rose from the depths of Tartarus with his vile demons solely for the purpose of gathering to personally torture you, and that their genuine intent of mental, emotional, and spiritual anguish is tearing you to shreds. Your heart weighs as heavily as leaden legs which you would drag yourself forward with if not for the quicksand that overcomes you, pulling you down inch by inch, paralyzing your will and threatening oblivion. And all the while fire and brimstone pour from the sky, pelting only you. Truly, that is what it feels like. But that feeling is a trial that won't last forever. Never give up.

~ Richelle E. Goodrich

Now that we know more about willpower, and hopefully, a little bit more about ourselves, how can we take what we know about willpower and apply it to our lives?

We've talked about several different situations that require willpower, so you know by now, that you need willpower for just about every situation in your life. As we said in the introduction of this book, willpower is the one thing that people wish they had more control over. Now you can see why. Your ability to create a successful and rewarding life depends on it.

Take what you've learned from the first part of the book about willpower: How it works, how much you have, what you can do to strengthen it. Then, take that and apply it to the ways you've learned to control your habits and emotions in order to live a happier, healthier life.

As author Norman Collins once said, "Free will and determinism are like a game of cards. The hand that is dealt you is determinism. The way you play your hand is free will." The choice is yours. Best of luck to you!

Thank you!!!
Can I ask
a favor?

Thank you so much for reading my book. I hope it both inspired and empowered you!

As you probably know, many people look at the reviews on Amazon before they decide to purchase a book.

If you liked the book, could you please take a minute to leave a review with your feedback?

60 seconds is all I'm asking for, and it would mean the world to me.

To leave a review, simply go to Amazon and click on "Your Account" option (which can be found in the upper right section under your name). Click on "Your Orders" and find this book.

Click on the button that says "Available Actions" and use the pull down arrow. Select "Write a Product Review" and tell others what you liked about the book in a few sentences.

If you want to reach me personally, please email me at ap@allisonperrybooks.com. I read all emails personally.

Thank you so much!

32641427R00061

Made in the USA
San Bernardino, CA
11 April 2016